Captain Eric Brown, CBE, DSC, AFC was Britain's first rotary-wing research test pilot. He made important contributions to vortex ring state and rotor airflow pattern research, and carried out the first recorded instrument (blind) flights in a helicopter. For this work he became the first helicopter pilot in the world to receive a decoration in recognition.

In 1970 he became Chief Executive of the British Helicopter Advisory Board, which is the representative body of the UK civil helicopter operations industry. He was elected to the Rotorcraft Section Committee of the Royal Aeronautical Society, and was its Chairman from 1973-76.

He took over as Secretary of the Helicopter Club of Great Britain in 1972, and organised the first British Helicopter Championships in that year, and the World Championships in 1973. The Helicopter Club is now a sporting component of the British Helicopter Advisory Board.

The Federation Aeronautique Internationale nominated Captain Brown as Chief International Helicopter Judge in January 1980.

In his capacity as Chief Executive of the BHAB, he was nominated to Chairman of the Helicopter Pilot Training Panel, which administered the successful government/industry sponsored helicopter pilot training scheme, producing 400 pilots for UK commercial operators over a five year period up to 1980/81.

Although a highly experienced helicopter pilot, Captain Brown is best known for his fixed-wing flying record as the Royal Navy's Chief Test Pilot. He holds many 'firsts' in naval aviation, including the first landing of a jet aeroplane on an aircraft carrier and the world record number of deck landings as well as types of aircraft flown.

The Helicopter in Civil Operations

Captain Eric Brown
C.B.E., D.Sc., A.F.C., M.A., F.R.Ae.S., Royal Navy

The Helicopter in Civil Operations

 **VAN NOSTRAND REINHOLD COMPANY**
NEW YORK   CINCINNATI   TORONTO   LONDON   MELBOURNE

Library of Congress Catalog Card Number 80-6227

ISBN 0–442–24528–9

Printed in Great Britain

Published 1981 by Van Nostrand Reinhold Company
A division of Litton Educational Publishing, Inc.
135 West 50th Street, New York, NY 10020, U.S.A.

First published in Great Britain 1981 by Granada Publishing
Frogmore, St Albans, Herts AL2 2NF
and
3 Upper James Street, London W1R 4BP

Granada ®
Granada Publishing ®

Contents

Preface   vii

Chapter 1   The present state of the art of helicoptering   1

Chapter 2   The capability of the helicopter   7

Chapter 3   The scope of the helicopter as a commercial   14
             vehicle

Chapter 4   The key role of the helicopter in offshore oil and   20
             gas exploration and production

Chapter 5   The aerial workhorse   31

Chapter 6   The flying crane   56

Chapter 7   The aerial Rolls-Royce   71

Chapter 8   The helicopter in public service   79

Chapter 9   Scheduled services   99

Chapter 10   The air taxi and the dual trainer   109

Chapter 11   Rotorcraft safety   117

Chapter 12   Environmental problems   126

Chapter 13   The economics of helicoptering   134

Chapter 14   The private helicopter   139

Chapter 15   The helicopter in sport   143

Chapter 16   The growing helicopter market   147

Chapter 17   Technological progress in helicopter development   150

Chapter 18   The future outlook for the helicopter   155

Chapter 19   The other side of the fence   162

Chapter 20   The last word   166

Civil helicopters — basic data   169

Navaids   175

Index   178

Preface

Many people persuaded me to write this book, unknown to themselves. These were the voices on the telephone of the British Helicopter Advisory Board, who wanted information of a general nature on commercial helicopter operations but could not find any comprehensive reference book. The final act of persuasion was that of my wife Lynn, who loves helicopters and hates to see me with too much leisure time on my hands.

The text is aimed at potential users of commercial helicopters, but I hope that commercial operators and aircrew will also find it both interesting and informative, because much of it is gleaned direcly from their experiences.

I wish to dedicate the book to Alan Bristow and Jock Cameron, two of the pioneers of commercial helicoptering, not only in the U.K. but world-wide. The three of us have known each other in the field of rotary-wing flying for some thirty-five years and I venture to say that in spite of the passage of time and the vicissitudes of the game, our enthusiasm for this splendid and exciting industry remains undiminished.

I trust that those who read through these pages will capture some of the feeling that they are in contact with a unique flight vehicle in an industry that is equally unique in the men it attracts, and for that reason must have a very bright future.

I owe much to the operators, manufacturers, aviation journals, and regulating authorities both in the U.K. and U.S.A. who have supplied me with photographs and information on which to draw, and I acknowledge their contributions with thanks. It is typical of the spirit of co-operation in the helicopter world that none has wanted special mention, since they felt that such a book will surely help the industry.

Eric M. Brown

Chapter 1

The present state of the art of helicoptering

The principle of vertical flight has fascinated mankind for centuries, and this interest was largely inspired by observation of birds, insects, and even the spinning action of leaves such as the sycamore.

Attempts to emulate these wonders of nature varied from simple children's toys, through theoretical tracts and models such as those of the Renaissance genius Leonardo da Vinci, to many weird and wonderful aeronautical contraptions which would have done credit to that master of the improbable – Heath Robinson.

The first practical helicopter is generally considered to be the VS–300, designed, built and flown in the U.S.A. by the great Igor Sikorsky, whose name is indelibly written into the history of helicoptering. Sikorsky's first controlled flight on 14 September 1939, showed the way ahead, and designs began to proliferate over the next decade, although they were plagued by lack of suitable engines, unreliability of the gearbox and transmissions, and high vibrations.

The early applications of the helicopter were confined to military tasks such as reconnaissance, gunnery spotting, communications, ambulance, and search and rescue. It was in this latter role that the helicopter made a world-wide impact, and even today the image of a 'flying lifeboat' is

Igor Sikorsky flying the VS–300

uppermost in the minds of the public when they think of a helicopter.

It was not till 1946 that the first helicopter received certification for commercial use, but its potential in this sector was slow in developing. The reason for this was basically because the helicopter really missed World War II, so it had to wait for the Korean War to get its first techological boost, and for the Vietnamese War to get the boom in technological progress that a major war inevitably brings in its train.

Even after the Korean War all commercial helicopters were direct adaptations of military types, and helicopter design of the 1960s was commensurate with the fixed-wing state of the design art of the 1930s. This combination of military hardware and immature design was hardly the formula for commercial success, so inevitably the graph of growth in the field of commercial helicoptering showed a shallow gradient for twenty years. In commercial terms the reasons for this slow civil development were (a) the high capital cost of the aircraft, (b) the high operating costs caused by demanding maintenance requirements, (c) poor payload capability, (d) lack of public awareness of the helicopter's versatility of operation and flexibility of role, and (e) lack of all-weather flight capability.

The event that changed this scenario was the Vietnam War with its vast deployment of helicopters. The resultant acceleration in technology to meet the demands of these military operations gave tremendous spin-off benefit to the civil element. In particular the introduction of the turbine engine into small 4/5-seat helicopters opened up a new era in commercial helicoptering.

The year 1970 probably marked the beginning of commercial helicoptering in its own right, with the onset of new designs aimed specifically at the civil market. At first these new helicopters were mainly of the small single turbine-engine 4/5-seat executive type, but at the same time the private market began to expand and the 2/3-seat piston-engine type began to appear in modern guise. The Bell Jet Ranger and the Enstrom F28A were the two helicopters most representative of these types, which began to appear in large numbers over the western world.

The U.S.A. were the leaders in helicopter design, and their new civil products began to reflect the styling of American automobiles – sleek and attractive yet luxuriously functional. Helicopters no longer looked like glass bubbles attached to a girder-like rear structure with a mass of open machinery in the middle. Lady passengers were no longer a rarity, thus demonstrating the new respectability of helicopter transport.

This new image also sparked off new civil designs in France, Germany, Italy and Great Britain, and each contributed something of the national inventive genius of the country. This competition was a healthy sign of a surge to break out of some of the shackles that had slowed up commercial acceptance of the helicopter.

The fundamental efficiency of the helicopter is not dissimilar to that of an equivalent fixed-wing aircraft. Basic fuel usage costs of the two types do not differ much, since the increased fuel consumption of the helicopter in flight is just about compensated by its direct landing and take-off, which avoids wasteful holding patterns and extended taxying.

The great advantage of the helicopter over its fixed-wing counterpart is its ability to operate from very small sites, because of its vertical take-off and landing capability. This fact of very slow take-off and landing speeds make the helicopter a potentially safe aircraft, for the take-off and landing phase is the most hazardous part of a conventional aeroplane's flight.

Additionally the helicopter can in the event of complete engine failure go into autorotation, when in effect it becomes a controlled parachute in descent and can make a zero speed touch-down. Autorotational flight is of course regularly practised by all helicopter pilots, and the panoramic view from the cockpit, which is a feature of every helicopter, makes this a relatively simple exercise.

Limitation of speed has in the past restricted the ranges at which helicopters can become competitive with aeroplanes in terms of block time, i.e. time from passenger arrival at departure point to passenger clearance from arrival point. These ranges in the mid-1970s were about 200–250 miles (320–400 kilometres), but should be nearer 400 miles (650 kilometres) by the mid-1980s. Since increased speed means productivity gain in commercial terms, there is now much more attention paid to drag reduction in helicopter design, by not only making body shape more streamlined, but by retracting landing gear, and achieving substantial drag reduction in the hub area of the rotor head – a notoriously messy area in early designs.

The major difference between fixed- and rotary-wing aircraft lies in the mechanical complexity of the latter. Massive rotating parts are used incorporating flap, lag and feathering hinges. These have to be driven at low rotational speed, and thus high torque, through a minimum weight transmission system. Such a system needs very regulated maintenance, and results in low overhaul lives of major components such as gear boxes. Overhaul lives of 250 hours or even less was the rule rather than the exception twenty years ago, but these times are now of the order of 2000 hours. Development in new fail safe features and new techniques may ultimately lead to 'on condition' overhaul life.

Early helicopters suffered from uncomfortable vibration, which was acceptable to the military, but was hardly a commercial asset. Likewise, noise, both external and internal was tolerated by military crews, but designers had taken little heed of fare-paying passengers or environmentalists. In the case of the latter this was probably because they are a rather modern phenomenon of mixed blessing as far as aviation is concerned.

These were not so much problem areas as areas of comparative neglect until civil helicopters became serious contenders for design attention. Now a vigorous technological attack is being mounted against these anti-social characteristics with inevitable success.

The way ahead for the civil helicopter has been bedevilled as much by economics as by technology. In the 1950s customers only called for the helicopter if it was apparent that no other tool could do the job. The costs of using helicopters were prohibitively high for any other approach to be taken other than dire necessity. However, this philosophy gradually began to change in the 1960s when it was demonstrated that the helicopters could offer advantages over other methods of doing the same job, and these advantages in fact meant real savings in terms of money. For example, the servicing of offshore oil rigs by helicopter rather than ship offers advantages in terms of time, reliability, emergency service and personnel comfort. In turn these factors aid personnel recruiting for offshore jobs.

Having burst out of the cocoon of commercial viability, the helicopter literally found that the world had become its oyster. There appears to be almost no limit to the versatility of this remarkable aircraft, and the proof lies in the study of the growth of helicoptering in the 1970s. However, it is a world of pitfalls for the unwary, and the pattern of commercial operations has formed itself into a sort of wheel layout with a comparatively small number of large, established operators forming the hub, and a very large number of small struggling operators forming the rim, while the spokes are those potential growth companies breaking out of the small-time and heading for the big-time. As the wheel of fortune spins many of those on the rim are cast off, and occasionally a spoke snaps, but replacements are always at hand, for helicoptering is an exciting game that attracts adventurous spirits.

The growth of the civil helicopter industry to its present level is one of almost imperceptible gain in the 1950s and then a fairly steady climb in the rate of growth in the 1960s, but in the early 1970s this accelerated considerably, and in Great Britain reached the astonishing rate of almost 60% in 1973. Since then the energy crisis and economic recession that have beset the world have slowed this uphill zoom to a sedate but healthy climb.

Paralleling this overall growth there has been a growth in the content of all-weather helicopters, which should have a pronounced impact on the future scene of rotary-wing operations. Since its inception the helicopter has basically been a visual flight aircraft with the pilot flying it by contact reference with the earth's surface. This limitation has largely been due to the poor inherent stability characteristics of the helicopter, which cannot be flown hands off, but it survived this shortcoming by virtue of its superb slow flying ability, which allowed it to feel its way along at low level in poor visibility or at worst land virtually anywhere if the weather deteriotated to mist or fog.

Instrument flight has been made possible in helicopters mainly by synthetic stabilisation, which is in effect a limited mode auto-pilot. However, the ability to penetrate cloud and fly without external visual reference has brought a train of technological problems such as icing protection and all-weather approach systems. Above all it has opened up exciting new vistas of flight operations for rotary-wing aircraft.

In general the basic concept of the helicopter has changed little in the forty years of its practical existence. There are still three main classifications:

single main rotor with torque-compensating tail rotor, tandem rotors with conventional rudder, and co-axial rotors with conventional rudder. The latter two classes are very much in the minority to the original Sikorsky layout of single main and tail rotors, which is popular on accounts of its relatively simple mechanical arrangement. Not that the other layouts are without their advantages, but these are too often outweighed by their disadvantages in commercial and military operations.

With regard to power-plants, the choice was restricted right up to the 1960s to piston engines, so that all the early helicopter designs which are still extant are in the main piston-engined, although a conversion to a turbine engine civil helicopters, although the situation should reach parity in 1980. By contrast there are virtually no multi piston-engine helicopters, although aircraft. However, the jet engine has now taken over in the field of medium and large helicopters and has infiltrated the small weight (below 2730 kg or 6000 lb) group.

In spite of the impact of the turbine engine on rotary-wing design, there are still more single piston-engine civil helicopters in the world than turbine-engine civil helicopters, although the situation should reach parity by 1980. In contrast there are virtually no multi piston-engine helicopters, although that is not to say there is no such requirement in the types spectrum.

Turbine engines have made their greatest impression in the public transport sector of helicopter operations, because they have contributed to speed, comfort and safety. The modern executive transport helicopter such as the Sikorsky S–76 is a revelation in this respect.

When comparing helicopters with other forms of transport it is necessary to establish a common basis of comparison, and a reasonable choice is a distance of 200 miles (320 kilometres), which encompasses the aeroplane, rail transport, automobile and bus.

A traveller over such a distance is normally interested in four factors: time, cost, safety and comfort, although not necessarily in that order. However, analysis of a large cross-section of the travelling public has shown that the majority do in fact place the factors in that order. If a table is composed giving points based on maxima of 20 for time, 15 for cost, 10 for safety and 5 for comfort, one gets an interesting comparison from interviewing 100 people with experience of all forms of transport.

	Time	Cost	Safety	Comfort	Total
Helicopter	20	3	4	3	30
Aeroplane	16	6	2	4	28
Rail transport	12	9	10	5	36
Automobile	8	12	6	2	28
Bus	4	15	8	1	28

Rail transport shows up strongly as best overall, followed by the helicopter. However, if one considers the two prime factors of time and cost only, the helicopter shows up best of all. It wins out on time, because of its doorstep to doorstep pick-up and delivery combined with minimal pre-flight and post-flight ground formalities, and a moderately high cruise speed. However, it costs about two-and-a-half times more than its nearest competitor, the aeroplane, so its cutomer appeal depends on cost effectiveness.

Perhaps one of the best examples illustrating the cost effectiveness of the helicopter in the transport role was that of the London-based chairman of a large manufacturing group with four major factories spread north of the capital at distances from each other of approximately 50 miles (80 kilometres). At regular intervals he was picked up from the garden of his home 20 miles (30 kilometres) south of London, then flown to London's heliport to embark with three of his executive staff, thence to each factory in turn for a one hour meeting before returning to London for a final hour of a normal day in the office.

This example pinpoints the strength and the weakness of the helicopter as a form of public transport. It offers unique versatility and flexibility of operation, but the seat per mile cost is outside the financial range of the ordinary traveller. The reduction of this cost represents a challenge to designers and commercial operators alike.

The main way ahead in the search for cost reduction undoubtedly lies with the design engineers, and proof of this lies in comparing the 25 pence (U.S. 50 cents) seat per mile cost of the Sikorsky S–61 design of the late 1950s with that of 15 pence (U.S. 30 cents) of the Sikorsky S–76 design of some twenty years later. In short, high technology spells low costs.

In practical terms the operator can only hope to make a direct contribution to reducing seat per mile costs by long-range operations, since this gives greater utilisation and also reduces the number of daily maintenance checks. Long-range helicopter operations only exist normally in scheduled type services such as are provided to offshore oil rigs, so the scope for the operator is somewhat limited.

To sum up, the present state of the art of helicoptering is that of a healthy, vigorous growth industry emerging from a chrysalis stage of technological development into an era of high technology, which offers the world a uniquely versatile and viable form of commercial transport.

Chapter 2

The capability of the helicopter

The fundamental flight characteristics of the helicopter cannot be emulated either by birds or any other mechanical vehicle. These characteristics should be understood at least basically if the unique versatility of the helicopter is to be fully appreciated.

(A) Hovering flight

During hovering flight in a no-wind condition, the main rotor tip path plane is parallel to the ground. Lift and thrust act straight up; weight and drag act straight down. The sum of the lift and thrust forces must equal the sum of the weight and drag forces for the helicopter to hover.

(B) Vertical flight

This is an extension of the hover condition: if the sum of the lift and thrust forces is greater than the sum of the weight and drag forces the helicopter rises vertically. If lift and thrust are less than weight and drag the helicopter descends vertically.

(C) Sideways flight

In sideways flight the main rotor tip path plane is tilted sideways in the direction that flight is desired. In this case lift still acts straight up and weight straight down, but thrust now acts sideways with drag acting to the opposite side.

(D) Rearward flight

Again lift still acts straight up and weight straight down, but thrust is rearward and drag forward – just the opposite to forward flight.

Although I have not mentioned forward flight, since this of course is taken for granted nowadays, it is interesting to note that Igor Sikorsky's VS–300 flew well in every direction except forward. When the president of United Aircraft mentioned that he had not seen it fly forwards like other aircraft, Mr Sikorsky replied 'Sir, this is a minor engineering problem that we have not yet succeeded in solving.' Fortunately this problem has now been solved.

Flight controls

The pilot has four controls to carry out these flight manoeuvres:

(a) *Cyclic pitch control:* This is in the form of the normal control column or 'stick' found in conventional aircraft. In the helicopter its purpose is to tilt the main rotor tip-path plane in the direction in which horizontal movement is desired.

(b) *Rudder pedals:* These are in the same form as on conventional aircraft, but they only control heading during flight manoeuvres (except in certain classes of helicopter fitted with a rudder when they control heading in all flight manoeuvres). In most helicopters they act as anti-torque pedals to counteract the torque effect of the main rotor. They are linked to a pitch change mechanism in the tail rotor gear box which enables the pilot to increase the pitch of the tail rotor blades. In forward flight in such tail rotor helicopters the pedals are not used to control the heading of the helicopter (except during portions of crosswind take-offs and approaches), but rather are used to put the helicopter in longitudinal trim so that slip or skid is eliminated. The cyclic control is used to change heading by making a co-ordinated turn to the desired direction.

(c) *Collective pitch control:* This control is peculiar to helicopters and is a lever or 'stick' located by the left side of the pilot's seat and is normally lying almost horizontal to the floor, moving up and down about the pivot at its aft end. Its function is to change the pitch angle of the main rotor blades. As the lever is raised there is a simultaneous and equal increase in the pitch angle of all the main rotor blades. The collective pitch control is the primary altitude control. In early two-seat helicopters this lever was situated between the seats, so that the first pilot sat on the right-hand side, and this custom remains to this day, in direct contrast to fixed-wing practice.

(d) *Throttle control:* This is normally mounted on the forward end of the collective pitch lever in the form of a motorcycle-type twist grip. Its function is to regulate engine and main rotor r.p.m. This co-ordination of power change with blade pitch angle change is controlled through a collective pitch lever/throttle control cam linkage, which automatically increases power when the collective pitch lever is raised and decreases power when the lever is lowered.

Helicopter aerodynamic phenomena

Superimposed on the fundamental aerodynamics of helicopter flight are certain phenomena peculiar to the vehicle, which have an effect on its handling and performance. A knowledge of these will aid full understanding of the capabilities of the helicopter.

(A) Torque

As the main rotor of a helicopter turns in one direction the fuselage tends to turn in the opposite direction unless counteracted by an anti-torque tail rotor, or obviated by use of a tandem rotors or co-axial rotors layout. The greater the engine power, the greater the torque effect.

(B) Gyroscopic precession

The spinning main rotor of a helicopter acts like a gyroscope when a rotor blade pitch change is made. Maximum reaction occurs approximately 90° later in the direction of rotation.

(C) Dissymmetry of lift

When hovering in still air, the lift created by the rotor blades at all corresponding positions around the rotor disc (area swept by the rotor blades) is equal. Dissymmetry of lift is created by horizontal flight or by wind during hovering flight and is the difference in lift that exists between the advancing blade half of the disc area and the retreating blade half. In effect, therefore, there are two unequal lift halves of the rotor disc and some compensation must be made to equalise these.

(D) Blade flapping

This is the method of compensating dissymmetry of lift by hinging the rotor blades at the hub attachment so that they can flap up and down as they rotate. The change in angle of attack on each blade brought about by this flapping action tends to equalise the lift over the two halves of the rotor disc.

(E) Coning

This is the upward bending of the main rotor blades caused by the combined forces of lift and centrifugal force.

(F) Drift

The entire helicopter has a tendency to move in the direction of the tail rotor thrust when hovering. To counteract this drift, the rotor mast in some helicopters is rigged slightly to one side so that the main rotor plane has a built-in tilt thus producing a small sideward thrust. Drift may also be overcome by rigging the cyclic pitch system to give the required amount of tilt to the main rotor plane.

(G) Ground effect

When hovering close to the ground the rotor blades displace air downward through the disc faster than it can escape from beneath the helicopter. This builds up a cushion of denser air between the ground and the helicopter, and aids in supporting the helicopter. It is usually effective to a height of approximately one half of the main rotor diameter. At approximately 3–5 m.p.h. (5–8 km/h) groundspeed the helicopter will leave its ground cushion.

(H) Translational lift

This is the additional lift obtained when entering horizontal flight, due to the increased efficiency of the rotor system. Translational lift is present with any horizontal movement although the increase is not normally noticeable until airspeed reaches approximately 15 m.p.h. (24 km/h).

(J) Transverse flow effect

In forward flight, air passing through the rear portion of the rotor disc has a higher downwash velocity than air passing through the forward portion. This in conjunction with gyroscopic precession gives an overall effect of a rolling tendency in the direction of rotor rotation on entry into effective translational lift where it may be accompanied by vibration.

(K) Pendular action

Since the fuselage on the large majority of helicopters is suspended from a single point and has considerable mass, it is free to oscillate either longitudinally or laterally like a pendulum. This is important in relation to blind flying when instruments give the pilot information on the position of the fuselage relative to the horizon; in fixed-wing aircraft this is synonymous with the position of the wings, but in rotary-wing aircraft the wings are in effect the main rotor and the position of fuselage and main rotor may not coincide.

Flight limitations

From the foregoing it will be appreciated that the helicopter is a complex aircraft to fly, but it is not a difficult aircraft to fly provided its idiosyncrasies are fully understood, as well as its operating limitations. Some of the latter are now worth a short study.

(a) *Centre of gravity limits:* The CG usually extends a short distance fore and aft of the main rotor mast. In helicopters the CG limits are much narrower than in fixed-wing aircraft, and indeed the range may be as small as 3 inches (76 mm). Thus weight and balance calculations are of prime importance to the helicopter pilot, as the position of the CG will affect the angle at which the fuselage is pendulously suspended from the main rotor. Tandem-rotor helicopters offer the advantage of a wider range of CG limits than single-rotor types.

Lateral balance is not normally a problem in helicopters since their fuselages are relatively narrow, and high sideways speeds will not be attained.

(b) *Retreating blade stall:* This is a condition that limits the forward speed of a helicopter, whereas in a fixed-wing aircraft the wing stall determines the low airspeed limits. In a helicopter the airflow over the retreating blade slows down as forward airspeed increases, whereas the reverse happens to the advancing blade. Since both blades must produce the same amount of lift the retreating blade angle of attack must be increased, and as forward speed increases this process will continue until the blade stalls. Warning of this impending condition is given by rotor vibration, pitch-up of the nose, and tendency to roll in the direction of the stalled side. There is normally a Vne (never exceed airspeed) placarded in the cockpit of every helicopter.

(c) *Power settling or vortex ring state:* This slow speed condition approximates to the powered stall in fixed-wing aircraft. It involves high vertical rates of descent, and the addition of more power produces an even greater rate of descent. Recovery is made by increasing forward speed and partially lowering collective pitch.

(d) *Ground resonance:* This may develop when a series of shocks cause the rotor head to become unbalanced. It is only likely to occur in helicopters of older design with fully articulated rotor systems and equipped with landing wheels. Initial ground contact on one wheel may set up the imbalance which is aggravated by further contact of one of the other wheels. It can develop very rapidly to the point of structural disintegration of the helicopter.

Corrective action by the pilot involves breaking the resonant mode by lifting the helicopter out of contact with the ground to eliminate the ground roll oscillations. If the r.p.m. are too low or other conditions prevent an immediate lift-off, the only alternative option is to close the throttle, but the r.p.m. decay rate may be too slow to untune the resonance prior to serious damage.

(e) *Dynamic rollover:* This is a threat when one landing skid or wheel is in contact with the ground while the helicopter is essentially hovering. During that transitional condition of near-hovering flight, the helicopter's roll inertia may be altered by the contacting landing gear in a dangerous fashion that effectively neutralises roll control authority by virtue of the fact that the helicopter will roll about the ground contact pivot point rather than about the centre of gravity, thus causing a marked change in the roll momentum. Once it has started, the rolling motion develops an inertia that exceeds the rotor system's roll authority and makes dynamic rollover inevitable.

Three conditions will induce unwanted roll: lateral centre of gravity offset, crosswinds, and fuel slosh, although the latter has only a minor effect. Therefore slope operations offer the greatest risk, although flat terrain with rutted or uneven surfaces can also initiate the problem by catching the gear.

Dynamic rollover is best corrected by using the helicopter's weight to destabilise the roll momentum, hence the pilot should lower the collective control lever rapidly to eliminate main rotor thrust and its roll vector.

Autorotation

This is the flight condition during which no engine power is supplied, and the main rotor is driven only by the action of the relative wind. The helicopter transmission is designed so that the engine, when it stops, is automatically disengaged from the main rotor system, thus allowing the main rotor to rotate freely in its original direction. In this condition the flow of air is upward through the freewheeling rotor as opposed to a downward flow through the rotor when under power.

This autorotation capability is used to safely land a helicopter after engine failure or certain other emergencies, although of course the pilot has to make some transitions to establish stabilised autorotative flight. These transitions will be at a minimum if the helicopter is in descent when engine failure occurs, and at a maximum if in a vertical climb.

For every single-engine helicopter there is an avoid area at low speed and low altitude in which there will be insufficient time to make the necessary full transition to autorotative flight in the event of engine failure, so that a heavy landing will be inevitable, but this area can normally be avoided by correct piloting procedures, and even if it has to be entered it will only be for a few seconds.

Each type of helicopter has a specific airspeed at which a power-off glide is most efficient. The best airspeed is that which combines the greatest glide distance with the slowest rate of descent. Turns can be made in autorotative descent, but generally only cyclic control should be used to avoid loss of airspeed and nose down pitch.

Helicopters with high inertia rotors have a glide ratio of about 4:1, while low-inertia rotors give glide ratios of the order of 3:1. As a rule of thumb a typical helicopter will glide a distance of 1 mile for every 1000 feet of height lost in autorotative descent (1 kilometre for every 200 metres).

Performance

Helicopter performance depends on air density, gross weight and wind velocity during take-off, hovering and landing.

As altitude increases the air becomes thinner and colder. Thin air reduces the amount of lift of the rotor blades and also the power of normally aspirated piston-engines, but increases turbine-engine efficiency. In general therefore increase in altitude reduces the hovering capabilities of the helicopter and particularly so if it is piston-engined.

An increase in temperature makes air less dense and thus will also decrease hovering ceiling. Similarly as the amount of moisture in the air increases, the hovering ceiling decreases.

The effect of gross weight on performance is self-evident. It is the one controllable factor of the many variables affecting performance. However, if the situation is reached in which the helicopter cannot take-off vertically there may be an alternative to reducing weight and that is to make a running take-off if terrain and type of landing gear permit.

Translational lift becomes really effective at an airspeed above 15 m.p.h. (24 km/h). Since translift is created by airspeed, not groundspeed, it is also present when the helicopter is hovering in a wind. If that wind is 15 m.p.h. (24 km/h) or more the helicopter will be experiencing effective translational lift in a hover, so less power is required to hover than would be required in a no-wind condition. The extra power available can be used to take-off with a heavier load.

To sum up on performance aspects, the most favourable conditions for a helicopter are the combination of a low density altitude (i.e. dense air), light gross weight, and moderate to strong wind. Needless to say these seldom appertain to commercial helicoptering, and that is why it is essential for the operator and useful for the customer to understand the capabilities of the helicopter. Familiarity can breed contempt so an occasional return to basics is good for every pilot's soul, and while ignorance may be bliss for the reluctant passenger it is not good commercial sense for the money-conscious customer. In both cases the old adage that 'you can never know it all' remains unquestionably true.

Although the principles have changed little, the standards of performance have progressed at a pace that is a steady trot rather than a gallop. The comparison given is of two types of helicopter at present in service in the commercial field.

	Bell 47	Boeing-Vertol Chinook
Year of civil certification	1946	1981
Classification	single rotor	tandem rotor
Engines	single piston-engine	twin turbine-engines
Crew + passengers	1 + 1	2 + 44
Max. take-off weight	2900 lb (1315 kg)	47 000 lb (21 300 kg)
Payload	1100 lb (500 kg)	25 000 lb (11 350 kg)
Fast cruise speed at 1000 ft	90 m.p.h. (145 km/h)	165 m.p.h. (265 km/h)
Range at max. weight	230 miles (370 km)	575 miles (925 km)
Max. range	300 miles (485 km)	725 miles (1165 km)
Rate of climb	800 ft/min (4 m/s)	2900 ft/min (15 m/s)
Service ceiling	9000 ft (2750 m)	15 000 ft (4600 m)
Hover in ground effect	4150 ft (1270 m)	15 000 ft (4600 m)
Hover out of ground effect	3000 ft (900 m)	14 700 ft (4500 m)

Chapter 3

The scope of the helicopter as a commercial vehicle

The slow start and halting progress of the helicopter in the 1950s and 1960s was mainly due to potential customers not realising the incredible versatility of the vehicle. There were of course other factors such as limited performance of the types then available, uncertain reliability, limitations on operating conditions, etc. However, the hard fact remains that marketing was the major flaw in the acceptance of the helicopter as a useful commercial tool. The public could clearly see the role of the helicopter in the military armoury, but saw little or no read-across to commercial application because they were neither informed nor educated by the industry itself.

All this has now changed because of an awareness by operators that they must sell their capabilities and not just sit and wait for manna to fall from heaven. This latter attitude has in some ways been encouraged in the past by lucrative contracts from oil companies falling into the laps of the few operators able to handle them, but when word got around about such bonanzas, the competition soon grew as new operators sprang into being, and public relations became a way of life as a result.

The United States of America as the seat of the helicopter industry was the first country to benefit, because its military forces did a superb advertising job for the helicopter in the Far East, but Europe was not far behind in spreading her rotary-wing commercial interests into the Middle East and Africa. Meanwhile American domestic influence was crossing the borders into Canada and South America.

While all this commercial activity was going on the Russians were not slumbering, and although they initially spread little beyond these satellites appended to their own vast country, they are now seeking pastures new particularly in the under-developed countries.

Potential markets

There are three main markets for civil helicopters in the next decade: energy related services, agricultural application, and construction. These are the areas of world-wide demand, and they are mainly associated with under-developed countries or open seas. The vast oil and gas resources of the world are largely located under water, while the continents of Africa, Asia and Australia as well as the sub-continents of Canada, South America and Russia have huge tracts of inaccessible or sparsely inhabited territory. With the world facing a population explosion and an energy crisis, there is only one way open for mankind, namely to make the most of existing resources and expand in the search for new ones. One of the best tools to help achieve this is the helicopter, which thrives on operations over difficult terrain.

Perhaps one of the earliest illustrations of the helicopter's versatility in this respect was its use from whaling ships operating in Arctic and Antarctic waters to spot shoals of the mighty mammals. This has now become an obsolete task, but unquestionably showed how the helicopter could increase the effectiveness of such an operation in spite of the environmental problems involved.

A more modern example is Canada's James Bay Project. Almost 1000 miles (1600 km) north of Montreal, the government of Quebec is in the midst of a 15-year 20 billion dollar hydroelectric project in the scrubland area between the forests of the south and the barren Arctic tundra. The project covers 68 000 square miles (176 100 km^2), and the total annual energy output will be 68 billion kilowatt hours. The associated power grid will comprise five lines stretching 3000 miles (4800 km) and requiring the construction of 9000 pylons. This massive undertaking could not have happened without the helicopter, since the nearest established road network ended some 450 miles (720 km) to the south of the site area when the project was initiated. At one stage in its development there were 67 helicopters employed on the scheme, and 25 000 flight hours were achieved in one year.

Although the main markets for helicopters are in the wilder areas of the world, there are also plenty of opportunities in the more sophisticated areas. Increased usage of helicopters as executive transport is likely, especially with all-weather capability becoming more common. Scheduled services should also have a resurgence as the right size of helicopter appears on the scene to make the economics of such services viable.

However, it is aerial work that offers the greatest opportunities. This comprehensive term covers a wide spectrum of tasks from crop-spraying to law enforcement, from filming to heavy lift. In fact the list grows almost daily as the depths of the helicopter's versatility are plumbed still further, and there seems no end to it in sight.

The league table of the top four national fleets of civil helicopters reflects both their economic position and the catalyst for the impetus they have received:

1. United States of America – oil   7000 helicopters
2. Union of Soviet Socialist Republics – agriculture   3500 helicopters
3. Canada – land developments   1000 helicopters
4. United Kingdom – oil   500 helicopters

Climatic effects on operations

The helicopter knows no boundaries to its probable deployment, but it is likely to be heading for some of the more extreme climatic and geographical areas of the world such as Antarctica, Siberia, the Andes, the Sahara, the Amazon, the Congo and the Atlantic Ocean. Indeed it is already probing some of these zones, and is already well established in the rugged areas of Alaska, northern Canada, Malaysia, the Rocky Mountains, the Atlas Mountains, the North Sea and the Gulf of Arabia.

The most adverse conditions for a helicopter are 'hot and high', but other difficult conditions are icing, turbulence, high winds, sloping terrain.

Climatic extremes present the greatest difficulties. Hot weather destroys lift and reduces engine power, so care has to be taken to make full use of wind and translational lift and to maintain maximum allowable engine r.p.m. near the ground. Hovering should be as low and as short as possible, and take-off acceleration made very slowly. Often running take-offs and landings may be required if load is not to be drastically reduced.

Hot climates are usually associated with sand and dust, the abrasive action of which is extremely damaging to engines unless air filters are fitted. However, helicopter transmissions are equally vulnerable, so ground running in such conditions should be kept to a minimum.

Cold weather improves engine power, but there are often problems in getting the engine started as oil congeals very rapidly in low temperatures and the electrical system suffers from condensation, which occurs so quickly. Condensation also affects the fuel, which has to be filtered before use. Static electricity builds up rapidly in cold weather, so the helicopter should always be earthed when fuelling and starting. However, the main problem is that crew efficiency drops with the temperature, and a good rule of thumb is to cease operations at $-35°F$ ($-37°C$), because at this temperature not only does the human element reach a crisis point in efficiency, but the metal also becomes brittle.

Icing

The helicopter is essentially a low altitude vehicle, which is unlikely to operate above 10000 feet, (3000 metres), except in exceptional circumstances. They are not pressurised aircraft nor is oxygen normally provided. Now the severest icing conditions occur in the altitude band of 10000–20000 feet (3000–6000 metres), so the helicopter's problem is ameliorated somewhat by its low level propensity. A study of world-wide temperature patterns shows that except in Arctic winter conditions the temperature up to 10000 feet (3000 metres) seldom drops below $-4°F$ ($-20°C$), so the helicopter by no means escapes the problems of icing, snow, and freezing rain.

Technically it is not too difficult to protect the helicopter engine down to $-4°F$ ($-20°C$), and the air intakes and inlets against ice shed from the fuselage and snow precipitation of 1½ inches per hour (40 mm per hour), but the real problem comes in protecting the rotor blades. The rotational speed of the rotor makes the tips rotate at high subsonic speeds, and this gives a kinetic rise sufficient to obviate protection against ice down to 23°F

($-5°C$). The flexing of the rotor blades also assists the shedding of light ice. however, build-up of ice on the fuselage will increase drag and so increase the power required to maintain cruising speed. Below 23°F ($-5°C$) any build-up on the rotors will increase the torque required to turn them, and so performance is penalised by any ice accretion giving loss of lift. Also because of the potential of asymmetric shedding of ice and the resulting imbalance of the blades, excessive vibrations can occur, which will necessitate a reduction in speed to avoid stresses in the control system.

If the helicopter does get into controllability trouble due to icing, it may also have trouble effecting safe autorotation because of ice build-up near the inner portion of the rotor disc disrupting the airflow in that region of the blades, which has a significant influence on autorotative characteristics.

The problem of helicopter icing may sound reasonably severe, but to put it in perspective its occurrence is comparatively low. For example on the extensive North Sea offshore support operations in relation to oil and gas exploration, less than 1% of sorties are aborted or abandoned because of icing, which mainly occurs between 0°C and $-20°C$ (32°F to $-4°F$).

Lightning

Lightning strikes on helicopters are rather scarce and damage is usually minor, although the damage potential is being increased by the use of new non-conducting skin materials on rotor blades, such as fibreglass.

Lightning ranges from 1000 feet to 100 miles in length (300 metres to 160 kilometres), with the most common type about one mile long (1.6 kilometres). The energy content of a typical stroke is about 400 million horsepower (3 million kilowatts). The return stroke – the visible part of lightning – travels at 328 000 feet per second (100 000 metres per second) and has a temperature of 50 000°F (27 760°C), five times hotter than the sun's surface, and can create a current as high as 200 million amperes.

There is a strong tendency for lightning strikes on aircraft to occur near the freezing level, and helicopter operations below this level are endangered only by cloud-to-ground strikes in the vicinity of developing thunderstorms.

The likely points of a helicopter to be struck are the tip of the main rotor, the tail rotor pylon, and the landing gear. The charge then exits through the landing gear to the ground, or through the tail boom to exit at the tail skid. Most skin damage is molten pitting, but antennas subjected to a strike will usually shatter, although the associated avionics equipment will continue to function with some impairment to performance.

Turbulence

Rotary-wing aircraft generally give a smoother ride in rough air than a fixed-wing aircraft of equivalent weight, because the rotor blades act as gust alleviators without transmitting the vertical accelerations back to the fuselage.

Although helicopters enjoy more tolerance to rough conditions than light aeroplanes, experience with military operations has indicated that severe turbulence is to be avoided, particularly as the fatigue aspects of turbulence on helicopter main rotor blades is a subject that is yet to be understood fully.

The kind of turbulence associated with mountain flying requires sound knowledge of the peculiar airflow characteristics of pinnacle and ridgeline operations. A pinnacle is an area from which the ground drops away steeply on all sides, while a ridgeline is a long area from which the ground drops away steeply on one or two sides.

If it is necessary to climb to a pinnacle or ridgeline the climb should be performed on the upwind side, when practicable, to take advantage of any updraughts.

A steeper than normal landing approach should be used when it is known that excessive downdraughts are likely to be encountered, but if it is suspected that the helicopter cannot be hovered out of ground effect then the load should be adjusted to allow a shallower than normal approach. The approach path to a ridgeline is usually parallel to the ridgeline and as nearly into wind as possible. If a crosswind exists then the helicopter should be kept clear of downdraughts on the leeward or downwind side of the ridgeline, and a low turn into-wind may be made just prior to touch down. Similarly on approaching a pinnacle the helicopter should avoid leeward turbulence.

Since pinnacles and ridgelines are generally higher than the immediate surrounding terrain, gaining airspeed on take-off is more important than gaining height.

High winds inevitably mean turbulence, but in addition they can limit operations if the helicopter has to start up or shut down in the open. There is a limiting windspeed for engaging or stopping the main rotor because at low rotational speeds the blades are still drooping and they may flail in winds above about 60 m.p.h. (95 km/h) and strike parts of the helicopter fuselage, particularly the tail cone. This situation can be overcome by starting up or shutting down in a hangar, but where the limitations are significant, such as in oil rig operations in areas like the North Sea, loading and refuelling with rotors running is common practice.

Winds of a lower velocity can still pose problems for helicopters operating in confined areas by creating turbulence around obstructions such as buildings or trees in leaf. The turbulent area near the ground is on the downwind side of the obstruction, and is always relative in size to that of the obstacle, and relative in intensity to the velocity of the wind. Turbulence can also be created near the ground on the immediate upwind side of any solid obstruction, but is not generally dangerous at wind velocities of less than 20 m.p.h. (32 km/h).

Slope operations

Sloping ground does not generally present any problems, although there are

The Sikorsky YUH–60A making a 15° slope landing

of course limits in the gradients acceptable. Normally a slope of 5° is about the limit. It is usually best for the helicopter to be landed cross slope rather than up slope. Landing down slope is not good practice because of the possibility of the tail rotor striking the ground.

Before landing in confined or mountain areas the circumspect pilot will make a high reconnaissance of the site at a height of about 500 ft (150 metres), and then a low reconnaissance on the approach, to check for wires, slopes, etc. that are difficult to see higher up. Similarly a ground reconnaissance before take-off from difficult sites is useful and indeed essential if the helicopter is to be flown rearwards from the landing position to the optimum take-off position, and the placing of ground reference markers will help in this respect.

In essence therefore it can be truthfully said that the helicopter can deal with almost any type of climate and terrain, sometimes with limitations in performance, but these are gradually being overcome by technology and improved piloting methods.

A company which has made a great contribution to world-wide operations, is Bristow Helicopters. Based in the U.K. this company operates what is virtually a commercial air force in size, specialising in offshore support operations but ranging all over the globe, and acquiring an international expertise second to none.

Chapter 4

The key role of the helicopter in offshore oil and gas exploration and production

Oil has changed the fortunes of men and nations alike. It is the life-blood of modern industry and transportation, and is synonymous in the minds of many with the Americanism 'bonanza'. Certainly it has proved to be the turning point in the short history of commercial helicoptering, and has for many civil operators indeed provided a bonanza.

The oil industry flourished without the helicopter for many decades until the law of supply and demand changed the whole scene. The world demand for oil became so vast, rising from 250 million tons (254 million tonnes) in 1920 to 2.3 billion tons (2.3 billion tonnes) in 1970, that supply was in grave danger of running out unless new sources could be found. Exploration was forced to move out to sea beds, jungles, deserts and other inaccessible areas of the world, and the unique versatility of the helicopter was inevitably utilised in this search for black gold, and today there are more helicopters operating in offshore support than any other helicopter activity, excluding the military.

There are three main offshore areas of helicopter activity, which together demonstrate what is involved: the Gulf of Mexico, the North Sea, and the Gulf of Alaska, covering a climatic span from the Arctic Circle to the Tropics.

Gulf of Mexico

There are some 6000 oil wells in the Gulf of Mexico, most in water less than 150 feet (46 m) deep, and all located west of the Mississippi delta. Each well costs eight times as much to drill as an onshore well, and the Gulf complex of wells is made up of about 1200 platforms. There are some 600 helicopters supporting these offshore platforms, moving at least 5000 people every day. The two major operators, Petroleum Helicopters and Air Logistics, are based at Lafayette, Louisiana, to serve the Gulf's offshore population of 26000 workers. Production is 21 million barrels of crude oil and 350 trillion cubic feet (10 trillion cubic metres) of gas monthly.

Most of the established rigs in the Gulf of Mexico are within 130 miles (210 km) of the shore, and the weather in the area is fairly predictable with relatively calm water. These two facts have meant that single-engine helicopters are widely used and these fly in visual contact conditions commonly called VFR (Visual Flight Rules). There are of course occasions when instrument-flight capability is useful in maintaining regularity of service.

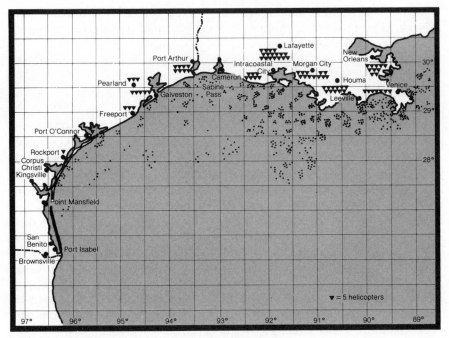

Helicopter offshore support operations in the Gulf of Mexico

This IFR (Instrument Flight Rules) capability is expensive to achieve in terms of equipment required to be fitted, and Gulf operators accept a small percentage of their helicopters being so equipped for safety reasons, such as night flights. There is also an inbuilt resistance to IFR by these operators because of the regulatory control it will bring in its train.

The IFR system used in the Gulf delineates specific IFR routes to rigs designated as IFR termini, where the helicopters either land or let down until they are clear to proceed VFR to another destination.

In general the Gulf of Mexico is the busiest civil helicopter scene in the world with 2 500 000 annual movements largely conducted in VFR, but with growing recognition of the value of an IFR capability.

North Sea

The North Sea presents a totally different picture, with a weather pattern so violent that IFR capability is essential, and only twin-engines safety is acceptable in offshore helicopter operations.

The North Sea's potential as an energy source was first tapped near the Dutch town of Groningen in 1962, when large quantities of gas were found underground with the implication that more lay under the shallow waters between East Anglia and the Continent.

Early in 1964 Britain passed the Continental Shelf Act vesting mineral rights in the Crown and signed the United Nations Continental Shelf Convention, thus establishing its claim to the shelf surrounding the island comprising the United Kingdom.

The first U.K. gas strike was made off East Anglia in 1965, and the first major oil strike off the north-east coast of Scotland in December 1969, so it is a modern story. North Sea oil was found to be 'sweet oil', i.e. low in sulphur content and therefore easily refined.

However, the North Sea is notorious for its weather vagaries, and because of the unfriendly environment it costs up to fifteen times more to exploit oil from the North Sea than from the desert, and its exploitation would have been impossible without helicopters to provide the offshore support services.

There are about 80 U.K. helicopters on North Sea support operations and another 20 from Norway, Holland and Germany. They carry out some 1000 flights per day to support an offshore population of about 15 000. The great majority of the helicopters are of the larger twenty-plus seat type required to cover the long ranges of 250 miles (400 km), while the medium ones cover the ranges up to 150 miles (250 km). The small five-seat types are used for the inshore rigs or are actually based in hangars on rigs for inter-rig hopping within the complexes of platforms serving large fields. These offshore hangars, which have also been used for certain two-blade medium helicopters, allow the machines to be sheltered and maintained in this rugged environment, where winds of 60 m.p.h. (95 km/h) are common and 100 m.p.h. (160 km/h) not uncommon.

The pattern of operations is to ferry the rig crews to and from the

A Bell 212 hangared on a North Sea oil rig

mainland as they work either 7, 10 or 14 days on the rig followed by the same period ashore. Then there are spares and supplies to be ferried, and the inter-rig carriage of underslung loads. In addition there is a twenty-four-hour availability for commercial emergencies and life-saving emergencies. The latter are covered by commercial operators under contract to support specific rigs, by military Search and Rescue (SAR) services round the British Isles, and by a commercial SAR contract to plug gaps in the military cover.

There are two major helicopter bases at Dyce Airport (Aberdeen) and Sumburgh Airport (Shetland Isles), where the oil associated traffic growth pattern has been phenomenal over the last five years. Helicopter passengers at Aberdeen were 40000 in 1973, 140000 in 1975 and is estimated at 200000 for 1980, making it the third busiest airport in the United Kingdom.

The North Sea offshore population numbers about 15000 and the utilisation of the large Sikorsky S–61N type helicopters averages around 1500 flight hours per year, while the medium types average about 1000 and the small types about 1500. The U.K. North Sea pilot strength is some 400, which means a crew ratio of about 5 pilots per large aircraft and 2.5 pilots per small one.

The matter of recruiting such a pilot force posed a problem since the only source was ex-military pilots, who were not leaving the armed forces in sufficient numbers to meet the demand. Although foreign pilots were initially

A British Airways Helicopters S–61N on a North Sea oil rig

recruited in small numbers to make up the shortfall, the U.K. government and the U.K. helicopter industry joined forces to set up a sponsored training scheme in 1975 to produce some 25 pilots per year by giving ab initio training to young school leavers and students in the age group 18–25. All pilots are subject to statutory Flight Time Limitations, which restrict their maximum flight hours to 900 per year.

The North Sea is split down the middle by an irregular imaginary line called the Median Line. On the eastern side of this line operate the helicopters from Norway, Germany and Holland, but the bulk of the oil and gas fields are on the western side supported from the U.K.

However, the Median Line only divides the continental shelf and there is in fact an operating overlap by the helicopters, which serve oil companies and not national governments.

In this multi-national situation, national policies to North Sea operations differ in the matter of air traffic control, aircraft equipment, rig helideck standards, etc., but the differences are now minimal as the logic of standardisation takes over.

The number of oil rigs in the North Sea varies considerably from year to year and the number of drilling, crane and pipelaying barges varies almost monthly, as exploration sites change and oil fields come on stream so that production rigs replace exploration rigs. Over the years 1977–78 the rigs numbered about 50 and the vessels about 20. From 1970 to 1980 a total of ten million passengers has been flown to and from these helidecks.

There are some 2000 helicopter movements per day to support this situation, and the concentration of U.K. activity in two major bases in the north and two minor bases in the south-east coincides with military aircraft training zones, so that a traffic conflict of major proportions exists in both areas. The worst problem is in the East Shetland Basin, and has been eased by the use of NATO radar at Saxa Vord in the Shetlands, while the East Anglian area problem has largely been solved by establishing a 'helicopter corridor' from the mainland to the main rig complexes. The procedures in this corridor provide vertical separation from sea level to 3000 ft (900 m) in IMC (Instrument Meteorological Conditions) and from 500 ft to 3000 ft (150–900 m) in VMC (Visual Meterorological Conditions). There are also Helicopter Protected Zones round each complex of three or more rigs throughout the North Sea. Within these HPZs a circle of radius 1½ nautical miles (2778 m) is drawn around each platform with tangential lines not exceeding 5 nautical miles (9260 m) in length connecting each circumference to its nearest neighbour. HPZs extend from sea level to 2000 ft (600 m) and may not be transited or entered without VHF radio clearance.

The average number of passengers carried on North Sea flights is 10, and this fact means that more medium size helicopters will come into use. On the other hand there is a requirement for a very large helicopter to carry a worthwhile payload out to ranges of 300 miles (500 kilometres) and beyond, so the pattern of types is undergoing a change, with the large S–61N type, which has been the backbone of North Sea operations, liable to remain static in numbers.

The levels of manning on each rig during the three phases of development are: exploration, 70 to 100; construction and hook-up, 200 to 600; production, 160 to 200, although such rigs might eventually be fully automated.

The helidecks on offshore platforms in the North Sea have to conform to certain standards laid down by the Civil Aviation Authority and certified by the Department of Energy. Any departure from these standards means that operational limitations will be imposed. The matter of helideck turbulence due to inherently poor design or alterations to the rig structure has resulted in new construction rigs having to be wind tunnel tested before a Certificate of Fitness is issued. A particular problem arises in the case of production platforms which have clusters of industrial gas turbines, whose exhaust plumes create a temperature rise and a high velocity air current, thereby causing danger to the helicopter from turbulence and engine ingestion of hot gases, which reduces power. These plumes are now delineated to the pilot by introducing colour into them, and a temperature reading is also given.

The U.K. has introduced Helicopter Landing Officers on offshore platforms and it is their task to ensure a state of readiness of the helideck to operate helicopters, to assist with passenger embarkation and disembarkation, cargo loading and unloading, refuelling arrangements and general safety precautions.

The passengers on North Sea operations are briefed by both the oil companies and the helicopter operators, and are supplied with survival clothing (immersion suits) in the winter months, and life-saving jackets at all times. Each helicopter carries one or two emergency dinghies, and a cabin attendant is carried on many occasions. All these helicopters are of course fitted with flotation gear sufficient to keep the aircraft stable enough in waves having a height/length ratio 1:15 to allow passengers to evacuate and enter dinghies. Keeping the rotor running aids the stability of the fuselage in the water after ditching, but the vital action in these circumstances is to launch the aircraft's sea anchor within five seconds of landing in the water.

The weather of course is the most vital factor in North Sea operations, and the main hazards are wind, sea fog, snow and ice. The prevailing wind is westerly and so outbound legs are often made at groundspeeds in the region of 200 m.p.h. (320 km/h). For this reason diversion airfields are often nominated in Denmark or Norway rather than back in the British Isles as this would mean returning at very slow groundspeeds.

Most North Sea transit flights are made under IFR and there has been more experience accumulated in this environment than anywhere else in the world. The helicopters are equipped with the Decca navigation system with its high accuracy and reliability in this area, VOR (VHF Omni-Range), ADF (Automatic Direction Finder), weather radar, radio altimeters, and VHF radio. HF radio was fitted in the earlier stages because the range of VHF communications was so limited at low level, but HF was subject to the vagaries of the ionosphere at such latitudes, and the problem has been solved by increasing VHF coverage with the installation of troposcat re-broadcast facilities on certain major rigs.

Instrument flight involves three stages: take-off, en-route, and terminal approach to land. The first is mainly a procedural process requiring a clearway to allow for an engine failure and subsequent single-engine climb out. At shore bases this is normally monitored by radar.

The en-route phase requires departure outside radar cover to be made on VOR radials to give lateral separation between aircraft. Vertical separation of 500 ft (150 m) between aircraft is achieved on the quadrantal system of aircraft true heading, but when within radar cover, it is based on Air Traffic Control instructions depending on the traffic situation. Throughout the entire flight the Decca area navigation system is used. This gives low fre-quency continuous wave transmissions from a series of chain stations and provides all-altitude coverage which is accurate to within a few yards right down to the ground, and the information is presented on a pictorial flight log display. Chain changes are automatic as are chart changes. Instrument let-downs can be made on Decca to limits of 250 ft (400 m) decision height and 650 yards (600 m) visibility.

Weather radar makes a useful contribution particularly at night or in snow conditions when the Decca system shows some deterioriation in performance. It is also useful as an obstacle clearance aid when used on the minimum scale during the later stages of the approach to a rig. All such radars used on the North Sea are X-band, which combines excellent weather detection with sufficient resolution to pick up oil rigs at sea.

Major rigs are fitted with NDB (Non-directional Beacon) and these are homed on to by ADF and used for a procedural let-down, with limits of 200 ft (60 m) above the platform by day, and 600 ft (180 m) above mean sea level by night, both in a minimum visibility of 1000 yards (900 m). Radio altimeters are used at this stage due to the uncertainty of pressure information from the rigs. At shore bases the standard ILS (Instrument Landing System) as for fixed-wing aircraft may be used, with limits of 200 ft (60 m) decision height and 325 yards (300 m) visibility.

The introduction of MADGE (Microwave Aircraft Digital Guidance Equipment) on certain rigs has given a reduction in approach limits to 150 ft (45 m) above the platform in 325 yards (300 m) visibility. Since only about 1% of all planned sorties are aborted because of fog, MADGE may seem an expensive luxury, but its offset approach capability, which allows let-downs to be made up to 500 ft (150 m) laterally from the helideck, gives a safety factor which the oil companies consider worthwhile to protect the huge investment that a rig represents.

The offset approach technique is in fact a breakthrough in instrument let-downs. In general, the S–61N is not flown on instrument approaches below 60 knots (110 km/h), as this is well above engine-out safety speed and is also a comfortable speed on instruments.

In the offset technique the helicopter is guided along a straight, three degree, horizontally displaced beam softened track, which bypasses the helideck by about 650 ft (200 m). The approach is of course over the sea and so the helicopter descends to decision height and flies level for ½ nautical mile (926 m), thus giving the pilot half a minute at low workload before reaching decision range at 975 ft (300 m). If good visual contact is made the pilot can leave the track in order to land; if not the guidance is followed up to 975 ft (300 m) from the helideck, at which point a missed approach procedure is initiated. The co-pilot will normally fly the approach while the aircraft captain looks out for a visual sighting of the helideck. On making such contact the captain takes over and executes the landing.

En-route radio calls are made every ten minutes and any break in this sequence initiates emergency SAR action, this is because in winter the survival situation is such that passengers and crew have to wear rubber immersion suits, without which in a water temperature of 50°F (10°C) life can only be sustained for about 1 hour, or ½ hour at 40°F (5°C).

Icing is a condition that is frequently met in winter in the North Sea and the S–61N helicopters have official clearance to operate between 500 and 5000 feet (150 and 1500 metres) in forecast light icing conditions and a minimum outside air temperature of 23°F (− 5°C). This clearance is conditional upon the installation of engine inlet iceguards, an ice detector device, HF antenna restraint, illuminated outside air temperature gauge, and functioning windscreen heating.

Although such clearance is sufficient to hold planned sorties aborted due to icing down to 1%, the operators have acquired such a vast amount of practical experience in this environment that they are seeking the clearance to be extended to allow operations from sea level to 7000 feet (2000 metres) in forecast moderate icing conditions and a minimum outside air temperature of 14°F (− 10°C). The main advantage accruing would be a possible easing of payload restrictions, but more could be lost on the swings than would be gained on the roundabouts if it meant the fitting of expensive – in terms of both cost and weight – rotor blade de-icing heating equipment.

The North Sea helicopters' record of reliability and availability is up to that of a scheduled airline, and this is truly a remarkable achievement, attained by meticulous safety standards, rigorous training, and development of techniques and equipment to combat the problems involved.

Training is difficult to fit into such an intensive pattern of operations, especially night flying in the summer months, when there are only a few hours' darkness in these northern latitudes. This situation has largely been eased by the introduction of S–61 simulators based at Aberdeen and Forus in Norway.

These simulators consist of an S–61N cockpit mounted on a six axes hydraulic motion system, which gives the pilot the same control responses as in actual flight. There is a visual attachment using a computer-generated image, which is presented on an infinity image display, and can show selected airports or oil rigs and their surrounding environmental features. Further realism is added by sound and vibration effects, and weather conditions can be varied at will by the instructor.

The instructor, who sits at his own panel at the rear of the flight deck, can introduce any one of 150 different faults, or a combination of several at the same time. An audio tape allows realistic Volmet weather reports to be recorded and co-ordinated with the actual weather conditions simulated for a particular approach and bases. A total of 600 individual radio aids can be reproduced.

The visual system can generate five light-point colours – red-orange, amber, green, yellow, and white. It has the ability to display curved strings of lights for taxiways and street lighting. There are sixty-four shades of grey, which make possible the representation of fields, mountains, buildings, maritime background, and other surface features in dusk or twilight lighting conditions. The unit can display 4800 lights and 200 surfaces at the same time. Visibility can be altered, as can cloud base and top height, and various effects can be imposed on the visual scene, such as scud clouds and ground fog. Even the visible parts of the rotor are simulated.

The virtues of the simulator are its consistent availability, which allows programmed training, its representation of emergency situations with repeatability and without risk, and its high annual utilisation potential of at least 3000 hours. On these bases it is a more cost effective method of conducting many elements of training than by actual helicopter flights.

The U.K. sector of the North Sea should yield 4 million barrels of oil per day (an oilman's barrel is 35 gallons (160 litres)) in 1980, i.e. 200 million tons (203 million tonnes) per year, which is twice Britain's needs, while the gas yield should be 8000 million cubic feet (225 million cubic metres) per day, i.e. about 1½ times Britain's consumption.

Gulf of Alaska

Another area of oil exploration which virtually depends for survival on the helicopter is the Gulf of Alaska. Its operational environment is comparable to that of the North Sea. As in the North Sea the Alaskan offshore drilling rigs are equipped with NDBs, but the signal received is so affected by static electricity in the helicopter whilst flying through snow, and the airborne magnetic compass performance is so affected by large magnetic anomalies and variations present in the operating area, that the NDBs are only used as a back-up to the primary TACAN (Tactical Air Navigation) navigation system. The TACAN system was selected because it is compact, and its accurate, dependable bearing and DME (Distance Measuring Equipment) range signal generated by a single transponder gave adequate line-of-sight coverage for the distances involved, which are generally considerably shorter than those in the North Sea. TACAN also operates in the 1000 Hz band, above the frequencies where most weather-associated interference and static difficulties are encountered.

The yield potential of the Gulf of Alaska is considered to be less than that of the North Sea, so it is virtually a smaller scale North Sea operation with almost identical operating equipment, techniques, and conditions.

Atlantic Continental Shelf

Probably the most exciting offshore challenge that lies ahead for helicopter operators is the exploration of the Atlantic Continental Shelf west of the Outer Hebrides islands of Scotland. By virtue of its annexation in 1955 of the volcanic rock known as Rockall, the United Kingdom has bid claim to a potential exploration area of 52 000 square miles (135 000 km²).

The support of drilling operations at possible ranges of up to 450 nautical miles (833 km) from the Outer Hebrides poses formidable problems within the likely time scale. The Sikorsky S–61N, which has been the backbone of North Sea operations, has a range of 400 nautical miles (740 km) with a payload of only six passengers so is obviously inadequate for the task. However, the establishment of a forward base on the small island of St Kilda, which lies 40 nautical miles (74 km) off the Outer Hebrides could act as a first stepping stone between the large islands and the rigs. A second stepping stone could be a redundant semi-submersible oil rig optimised to be completely unobstructed, and fitted with refuelling and basic servicing facilities as well as some accommodation beneath the landing platform.

If two such floating helistops were introduced between St Kilda and the farthest rig complex, then the stages could be cut to 150 nautical miles (278 km) or less. However, there still remains the problem of diversion airfields. Since obviously no return to the mainland can be made, the helistops and the rigs themselves offer the only alternate landing sites, so they must all be equipped with an all-weather approach aid such as MADGE, and the helicopter must have single-engine hover capability in case of an engine failure. The S–61N has no such performance capability, so the task may rest with newer types such as the Puma or the Chinook. The Puma will be able to cope with the 150 nautical miles (278 km) stages, but the Chinook offers much greater range and payload capability.

Decca can still serve as the main en-route navigation aid in the Atlantic area, with VOR and ADF as secondary navaids. However, communications may pose a problem since VHF is a line-of-sight facility and therefore the helicopters may have to fly at greater transit altitudes than in the North Sea. This in itself could raise further problems, for it will mean flying into stronger winds on the outbound legs, and it will also increase the likelihood of being at heights where the risk of icing is higher.

Certainly in this type of environment reliable meteorological information will be all-important, so it may be necessary to position a weather ship in the area as well as station trained meteorological observers on all the rigs and possibly on the helistops.

The type of rig to be used in the Atlantic will have to have its own small helicopter hangared aboard, to undertake inter-rig transfers of men and equipment and also for emergency SAR duties. It would probably be a useful tool for checking and calibrating the landing aids and navaids sited on the rigs.

The drilling depths in the Atlantic Continental Shelf are likely to be about three times those of the North Sea, but the state of the technology is such that this should present no insurmountable problems. However, it will mean that the cost of Atlantic oil will be very high, but that will not be a deterrent in a world where oil is an essential but rapidly declining commodity. Certainly without helicopters the Atlantic game cannot be played, so it will present perhaps the greatest challenge yet to both the oil and the helicopter industries.

World-wide operations

Present estimates place current recoverable oil reserves at a minimum of two trillion barrels world-wide, but this may well prove to be an underestimate in the light of recent discoveries in Mexico.

The use of the helicopter in support of the oil industry is of course not just in offshore locations, but also on land such as in Indonesia, where it has been estimated that without the helicopter to cope with the dense jungle area the country's oil production would be reduced by half.

In South America there are about 150 helicopters supporting the oil and gas industry. Of these 90 are used on shore and 60 offshore. However, the potential of Brazil's vast jungle is relatively untapped, as are the waters between southern Argentina and the Falkland Islands.

Off the shores of the remote and wild Tierra del Fuego, seven oil rigs are serviced by Schreiner Helicopters, a Dutch company whose single Dauphin 2 flew 990 hours in eight months (May 1979–January 1980) in very adverse weather conditions. The number of rigs is increasing.

Another great challenge to the helicopter could lie in the Antarctic, where oil and gas are probably located offshore rather than under the continental ice sheet, but operations could embrace both land and sea.

Perhaps the most daunting prospect for oilmen lies off Canada's eastern coast. The Labrador Sea has a short drilling season of three months, and the area in winter abounds in icebergs like high-rise buildings and reaching over 1000 feet (300 metres) beneath the surface. Helicopters not only have to service the rigs, but spot icebergs, and be ever at the ready for emergency evacuations, and all this in the area of the notorious Newfoundland weather. As challenge indeed that demonstrates the key role the helicopter has to play in the energy industry.

The mystery question in the world-wide scene is whether any large oil and gas reserves lie off the coast of China, and whether the Chinese have the know-how to recover it if any exists. Certainly their commercial helicopter expertise would seem unlikely to be of the order required for offshore support services, so a potentially considerable market could be looming in this Far East area for Western operators.

Chapter 5

The aerial workhorse

The truly amazing versatility of the helicopter harnessed to the needs of man has earned it the title of 'the aerial workhorse'. The term 'aerial work' covers a tremendous spectrum of tasks, which are growing in variety from year to year, but it implies the commercial use of helicopters in non public transport roles. As a guide to a more precise definition of aerial work, it is fundamental that all persons carried in the helicopter on such work are acting as crew by contributing to the task involved.

A selection of these multifarious tasks is now examined to illustrate the flexibility of the helicopter in meeting the demands of modern life.

(A) Agriculture application

The world population is expected to double by the year 2000, and if it is to be fed adequately then agricultural productivity will have to be commensurately increased. One sure way of increasing yield is by fertilisation and pest control, and in these operations the helicopter plays a most effective role.

Fixed-wing aircraft have been used in aerial applications for some sixty years but the helicopter offers considerable advantages over the aeroplane, and so crop-spraying was one of the earliest commercial uses to which rotary-wing aircraft were put. The advantages offered by the helicopter are:

(a) It can be based closer to the site of the operation, thus saving turn-around by a considerable amount. Modern helicopter companies move a nurse truck onto the site to act as a mobile operations centre complete with its own helipad. There may also be a fuelling vehicle and chemical loader, although fuelling from barrelled fuel is common practice in the field. On-site operations also allow the grower closer involvement.
(b) It can fly lower and follow rough terrain more easily and thus ensure a more even distribution. The helicopter is blessed with outstanding pilot view and very low landing gear and flies comfortably at six feet (two metres) above the crop to be sprayed.
(c) Rotor airflow enables the underside as well as the topside of foliage to be effectively sprayed.

Crop spraying is a demanding task and one that is not very popular with pilots because it is seasonal, dangerous, and relatively low-paid. In consequence a sector of helicopter operations that requires experienced pilots tends anomalously to get low flight time pilots.

Obviously agricultural aviation booms in the summer months and declines in the winter, so the flying is intensive during the long daylight hours of summer. Turn-round times become vital in getting the task done, especially so in the case of the helicopter competing with the aeroplane, which normally carries a larger load of chemicals and flies faster. On-site helicopter turn-round times of 1 minute 15 seconds are not unusual, so the ground support team has to be as highly trained as the pit team supporting a grand prix racing car. In consequence the life of an agriculture pilot in the high season is one of intensive activity and little socialising.

The job of crop-spraying is dangerous because it involves flying with small margins for error in an environment that is often akin to that of an obstacle course, with trees and wires placed in a confined manoeuvring area. The accident rate is higher in this sector of helicopter operations than in any other, although the fatality and injury rate is surprisingly low, because the helicopter only flies at speeds between 30 and 60 knots at a small vertical distance from the ground, and the pilots normally wear protective helmets and anti-flash flying clothing.

Another danger to agriculture pilots is the risk of contamination from the chemicals they are working with. In particular organo-phosphorus contamination can have serious harmful effects on vision. Therefore all flights are made with the cockpit fully enclosed even in the tropics.

The rates of pay of agricultural pilots are largely dictated by the fact that the pilots have low experience in terms of flight hours, require no special skills such as instrument flying ability, and are in a business where the profit margins are eaten away by high insurance rates and are particularly subject to the vagaries of the weather.

The method of crop spraying by helicopter requires a 360° reconnaissance flight around the site at a height of about 200 feet (60 metres) to get an idea of the contour of the terrain and pinpoint obstructions such as trees, markers sticking up out of the crops, and so on. Then the pilot flies a diagonal pattern to check if anything was hidden in shadow.

Wires present a particular hazard, and collision with wires is the largest single cause of agricultural helicopter accidents. Grid power lines are thick enough and usually well enough marked on topical maps to be easily avoided, but it is the lower slung, thinner telephone wires or localised power lines that present the major danger. The matter of conspicuity or how to make wires more readily visible is a matter of much research but no perfect solution has been reached.

The actual spraying process is made at a height of about six feet (two metres) above the standing crop at speeds between 30 and 60 knots. The higher speeds are normally used for dry material applications. A normal application rate is 60 to 100 acres (25–40 hectares) per hour. The swath runs are made following markers, usually flagmen, and the turns at the end of each run are the most critical manoeuvre. The helicopter has to be pulled up into a sort of stall turn, which requires considerable judgement since the turn

A Bell Jet Ranger fitted with spray equipment

must be tight enough not to overshoot the next swath, and yet too sharp a pull-up may put the tail rotor into the crop, and too gentle a pull may put the spray booms into the crop during the turn. The wind strength and direction are of course vital factors in this operation, both with regard to manoeuvring and containing the dispersed chemicals within the confines of the field. A major factor in spraydrift is droplet size, which can be controlled by varying the pressure through the spray system.

The application of solids is often done from underslung hoppers, but this is area work used mainly in forestry as it is difficult to control chemical drift from the height required to fly at with an underslung load. The hoppers eject the solids by impellers driven by hydraulic power or integral gasoline engine.

The most popular models for agricultural work are the small two seat piston-engined Bell 47G, Hiller 12E, and to a lesser extent the Hughes 300 and Enstrom F28. The Bell 47 has even converted to a specialist single-seat agricultural version with a design configuration that saves 400 lb (180 kg) providing a payload of 800 lb (360 kg) even with mounted spray gear and enough fuel for a range of 150 miles (240 km). The use of larger helicopters has in the main been confined to forestry spraying, which involves larger areas with more room to manoeuvre.

The popularity of the Bell 47 and Hiller 12 largely rests on their ruggedness, reliability, and relatively good power/weight ratio. However, a conversion of these elderly types to turbine engines has recently been made, and there are protagonists of both schools of thought in the piston versus turbine engine argument for agricultural work. The advantages of both types of engine are listed below, assuming they are in the same airframe.

In general piston-engines are favoured in agricultural work for their greater cost effectiveness. The extent of this propensity may be gauged from the fact that there were 1000 agricultural helicopters in the U.S.A. in 1977,

An Aerospatiale Lama carrying an underslung hopper

Piston	Turbine
Cheaper to operate.	Has more power and therefore lifts more chemicals.
If supercharged, better performance above 10 000 ft (3000 m) altitude.	Greater crash safety as jet fuel is less volatile.
More responsive engine control for pilot.	Less pilot workload, as it has better throttle/r.p.m. synchronisation.
	Greater logistics problems such as large stocks of jet fuel required in the field.

of which 83% were piston-engined. However, there is a factor influencing this situation, which is often not considered. The vast majority of agricultural helicopters are Bell 47s and Hiller 12Es, which are no longer in production. Operators have been able to supply their needs from a large stock of second-hand models from the armed forces at very favourable purchase prices and this has helped to tip the cost effectiveness scales quite markedly.

Probably the classic employment of agricultural helicopters occurs in New Zealand, where 78% of the country's 66 million acres (27 million hectares) cannot be worked by wheels. Of the 43 million acres (17 million hectares) of occupied land, 66% are too steep and hilly for normal ground implements, but are capable of being turned into pastoral farming land if it could be fed top dressing, fertilised, and cleared of the pest rabbit population.

This task has now virtually been totally achieved by the use of agricultural aviation aircraft, in which helicopters have made up almost half the total numbers used. Perhaps the most astonishing feature is the annual utilisation rate of 700 hours per aircraft compared with about 220 hours average in the U.S.A., Canada, and the U.K.

Strangely enough in the inflation period of the mid-1970s agricultural application costs were falling, due largely to technological advances in both helicopter performance and spraying equipment design. Fertiliser can now be applied at rates of over 3000 lb (1361 kg) per minute, and 600 metric tons (tonnes) of phosphate were applied to the forests of Scotland in three days at a rate of 20–25 trips per hour. All this efficiency has made agricultural work one of the most profitable sectors of helicopter aerial work on a revenue for hours worked basis although costs to the customer would fall dramatically if low aircraft utilisation was doubled.

However, agricultural work has two great drawbacks from the operator's point of view – it is seasonal and it aggravates environmentalists. On the first score it means the operator must find back-up off-season work, and on the second it means he must spend much time educating the public and training his pilots in public relations.

Despite the growing importance of agricultural aircraft in crop production and crop protection there are many other uses for them in the development and management of biological resources, such as the control of locusts, the tsetse fly, malarial mosquitoes, and other insects of medical importance. Indeed the helicopter makes a splendid tool in applied ecology.

Many new techniques have been developed in agricultural aviation, such as helicopter hydroseeding of reclaimed surface mines. In this latter respect a hydro-spyder system has been developed, which provides uniform distribution of seed and fertiliser, and is unsurpassed in its ability to bind these materials to soil on steep slopes.

Another interesting use of helicopters is for frost protection of citrus fruits by employing the helicopter downwash at first light to remove the dew from the fruit before it can form into frost. Sometimes even earlier precaution is taken by flying the helicopter slowly at night at a height of 60–100 ft

(20–30 m) above ground level to force the warmer upper air down on to the surface.

In addition to these newer types of application there are the well-established granular coverage, dusting, fogging, and insecticide-fungicide-herbicide spraying.

The techniques used are mainly wide swath (high/medium speed) and narrow swath (contour flying at low speed). Swaths across a field can be marked with permanent flags if a field is to be treated several times a season, but the traditional swath marking is done by a flagman, who paces off the number of steps to each swath according to a prearranged swath width. He stands at each swath holding a conspicuous flag until the helicopter has made its run, when he steps off the distance to the next swath. However, the flagman's days seem numbered, as an array of electronic positioning systems come on the market. With a high degree of accuracy, these systems reduce chemical wastage through overlap and thus offer considerable cost benefits.

The agricultural helicopter is in effect an airborne tractor, which can enter a field irrespective of ground conditions without damaging the crop, thus reducing manpower and eliminating soil compaction caused by heavy machinery. Soil compaction in a wet year can require a three year recovery period.

There are some 20 000 agricultural aircraft in the world, of which about 5000 are estimated to be helicopters, with the ratio changing annually in the helicopter's favour. The U.S.A., Russia and Poland have been the leading countries in developing both agricultural aircraft and specialised distribution equipment.

(B) Aerial photography

The helicopter's entry into the field of aerial photography was slow, because it did not offer the stable, vibrationless platform so essential to good repro-ductive clarity. This situation was aggravated in early helicopters by their inability to hover out of ground effect to give motionless flight at an altitude where the camera could obtain ample ground coverage for area 'stills'.

The impetus to improve this situation was given by the interest of cinematography in the use of the helicopter to produce unusual angles or exhilarating action sequences. The technology of the film industry was brought to bear on the aerial problem, and resulted in specially designed inertia mounts that can isolate film and video cameras from helicopter vibrations and movements. The mounts have five axes, three main ones corresponding to a helicopter's pitch, roll, and yaw; two others at the camera portion, one for panning horizontally and the other for panning vertically. The camera equipment is very sophisticated, and the cameraman is a specialist in aerial photography.

The pilot too must be a specialist to understand the finer points of the filming game, and he is a vital part of an airborne team together with the cameraman and director. These three crew members are in touch on an inter-communication system, and the pilot is in radio contact with the ground.

The pilot is the key man in the team, for his appreciation of the task can make life easy for the cameraman. He should be able to assess things like the likelihood of rotorwash dust coming into view, or the shadow of the helicopter falling across the action, and when to accelerate or slow down to keep the subject in full view. An expert pilot and an inexperienced cameraman will always be a much superior combination to an expert cameraman and an inexperienced pilot

In 1976 it was calculated that some 10000 hours were flown on aerial photography world-wide. This is not a lot when spread over a large number of operators, and in consequence such work is considered as back-up revenue. The two main Los Angeles based inertia mount developers and suppliers have agents based around the world, who hire out the equipment on a lease basis, but other countries such as France and Britain have also developed similar equipment.

There is no doubt that the advent of the turbine-engined helicopter came at the right time to marry up with the inertia mount and give a smooth filming platform and it also provided speed performance to give the required margin of flexibility for action shots as in a high-speed car chase.

The field of aerial photography is expanding outside the cinema, to T.V. movies, documentaries and commercials, and of course there remains the steady demand for stills of almost anything you care to mention on the surface of the earth.

(C) Press and T.V. coverage

The media has developed the use of the helicopter in news coverage to the point that it is a vital tool of the trade. It can carry reporters and photographers to the scene of a newsworthy incident with alacrity and precision. It offers unrivalled aerial views at an altitude, which allows great detail to be discriminated by the human eye or camera.

Probably the greatest asset offered by the helicopter is its ability to take the newsmen to otherwise inaccessible places, where so often the action takes place, e.g. shipwrecks, cliff accidents, forest fires, etc. Natural disasters in particular are best covered by helicopters, e.g. avalanches, earthquakes, floods and volcanic eruptions.

The photography under such circumstances is of course by hand-held camera or cine-camera and is subject to helicopter vibrations and movements, but newsreel photography is generally accepted as being a grade below professional cinematography. Commercially, newsreels depend on live shots and not aesthetic photography.

Television newsreels usually cover sports events of a type that are particularly suited to aerial viewing. A classic example is the famous Oxford–

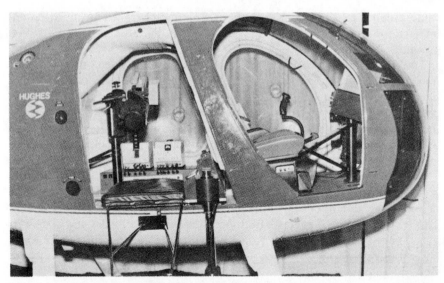

ENG Helicopter T.V. System aboard a Hughes 500D

Cambridge University Boat Race along the winding River Thames. Such live coverage is made possible by a gyro-stablised colour television camera mounted outside the helicopter in a rotatable sphere and operated by remote control by the cameraman sitting alongside the pilot. It is equipped with a 20 power zoom lens, and a microwave transmitting omnidirectional antenna permits the helicopter to manoeuvre without impairment to the broadcast. The antenna is retractable and is housed for take-off and landing. The unit also incorporates a microwave amplifier, and video tape recorder. It can beam pictures 150 miles (240 km), and can also relay pictures from ground units.

Some radio and television companies provide helicopter traffic surveillance reports at peak traffic periods for their listeners. These are very popular with car drivers listening on their car radios, as they can provide valuable information on accidents, traffic jams, diversions and alternative routes to avoid delays.

In news coverage, speed is of the essence in getting both reports and picture to press, and some major newspaper offices have rooftop helipads so that the material can be flown in direct.

Press and television news work is spasmodic, and indeed press work is regarded by helicopter operators as on an opportunity basis. Television events, however, are contract work and are usually very profitable.

(D) Power line inspection

Modern civilisation depends critically on electrical power, and the main electric grid system is therefore the nerve network of developed countries.

A Bell 47J on powerline inspection

The pylons and 400–500 kV power lines that make up this network are vulnerable to the vicissitudes of both nature and man. The corrosive effects of weather, lightning strikes, tree falls, high winds, strikes by model aircraft, stone throwing at insulators, are just a sample of the hazards that beset power lines. Inspection is therefore vital to detect faults before breakdown occurs.

The modern method of inspection involves a thermovision system where the line is scanned by an infra-red scope that shows up hot spots and other conductivity weaknesses provided the lines are at least half the maximum electrical loading and not cooled down by weather. The equipment incorporates a camera that can take a photographic record of any fault it is desired to analyse. The system is operated by an observer sitting behind the pilot with the scope and camera aimed out of a side window, while the helicopter is flown in parallel to and offset from the power lines. Another observer sits alongside the pilot and logs the pylon numbers and fault locations either in writing or by a cassette recorder plugged into the headset system. The helicopter flies just above power line height at 260 ft (80 m) distant with a speed of 60–80 knots (110–150 km/h).

Some electricity authorities also carry out inspection of the local supply lines of 11–33 kV. These are carried on wooden poles about half the height of the 180 ft (55 m) high pylons, and are inspected visually by an observer sitting alongside the pilot. This observer also has a hand-held infra-red scope available if required for more detailed inspection.

The 750 Aga system infra-red equipment (weight 5.5 kg) incorporating superviewer, 35 mm camera, and video camera (optional)

Two-hour patrols of some 130 miles (210 km) are usually flown, and a pilot will make three such flights in a day. Grid work usually calls for a turbine-engined helicopter, while local lines will normally be patrolled by small piston-engined types.

Power line inspection is year round contract work and is eagerly sought after by operators, although many electricity authorities now have their own helicopter units. The immensity of the work can be realised by the fact that the U.K. grid system covers 8000 miles (12 800 km) and is split into five regions. However, the cost of the surveying operation is cheap to the taxpayer or ratepayer compared with the financial penalties inflicted on the economy by a major power breakdown.

(E) Pipeline Inspection

Europe is a heavy consumer of gas as an energy source, and the discovery of North Sea gas has increased usage and reduced the price. In consequence maritime countries such as the United Kingdom and France each have some 10000 miles (16000 km) of gas pipes, of which some 3000 miles (5000 km) are the high pressure national transmission system and the much larger network comprises subsidiary low pressure gas pipelines directly supplying industrial and domestic users.

North Sea gas is brought in from the subsea fields at a pressure of 2000 lb per square inch (14000 kN/m^2), and is partially purified by removing the heavier hydrocarbons. It is then taken over by coastal terminal, reduced in pressure to 1000 lb/in^2 (7000 kN/m^2), provided with an unpleasant smell, and moved on to the national grid by a series of compressor stations sited every 40 miles (65 km). Their function is to keep the pressure constant in the 36 inch (91 cm) diameter pipes.

The British Gas Corporation has the whole 10000 mile (16000 km) network patrolled every two weeks, but this is a frequency not necessarily followed by other nations. However, things can happen with amazing rapidity which can effect a system capable of becoming potentially very dangerous if ruptured.

The patrol is made normally at a height of 300 to 500 ft (90–150 m) except over built-up areas where it is increased to 1500 ft (450 m). The pilot follows a series of markers indicating the underground pipeline, and tries to keep the line to the left of the helicopter so that the gas company observer sitting beside him can get a good lookout. The observer is looking for leaks, which can be detected by discolouration of the vegetation, encroachment by construction vehicles such as excavators or by foliage. Any construction work adjacent to pipelines has to be notified to the gas authority and may only be undertaken after issue of a permit by that authority. Another problem is land subsidence due to heavy rain shortly after a pipeline section has been laid.

Offshore oil has led to underwater pipelines from sea wells to shore storage and thence by land pipelines to tanker terminals and refineries. Oil pipelines are of a different nature from gas pipelines, in that they present a pollution risk rather than an explosion risk in the event of rupture. They are also laid in fairly straight lines between pumping stations, so that the system is easier to patrol than the spaghetti network of the gas lines. However, they have one feature that does not plague gas pipelines, and that is their attraction as a target to terrorist activities or vandalism.

Pipeline inspection is an attractive contract since it is normally steady bread and butter work. The British Gas Corporation contract involves over 4000 flight hours per year, and the network is of such complexity that it is usually divided up into geographical regions surveyed by different operators, who may vary from major to minor in fleet strength.

(F) Water sampling

The helicopter is not normally required to take water samples of reservoirs and inland lakes, but is used mainly for sampling in river estuaries and coastal waters. The process is required by water authorities as a check on pollution levels caused by sewage and industrial effluents.

The helicopter carries a water authority observer, who lowers a cassella with the helicopter hovering 5 feet (1½ metres) above the water surface. The cassella is in effect a bottle within a bottle, and the inner bottle thus acquires a water sample devoid of oxygen intake for analysis of pollution.

The European Economic Community has laid down standards for bathing beaches, which will require constant monitoring for pollution, so water sampling with its small beginnings has grown to offer good contract potential.

(G) Lighthouse relief

For island nations such as Great Britain, shipping is the country's lifeline, and the protection of that lifeline is vital to survival. Most coastal regions throughout the world therefore have lighthouses to warn shipping of hazards to navigation, such as rocks, reefs, shoals, etc.

Recruiting in the lighthouse service has always been affected by the uncertainty of relief in emergency such as sickness, or at set times such as rejoining one's family for Christmas, because of the inability of boats to reach storm-bound lighthouses. Now the helicopter has changed all that to the benefit of everyone concerned.

The famous old Trinity House Lighthouse Service in England employs a Bolkow 105D twin-engined helicopter, which performs the relief of fifteen lighthouses and nineteen lightvessels every twenty-eight days. Three keepers are exchanged on each lighthouse relief, and five crew members at each relief of a lightvessel. Approximately 675 lb (300 kg) of gear and provisions are carried on each relief flight for the men's monthly turn of duty. On average Trinity House charters its helicopter for 70 hours a month, during which time about 300 people use it.

Each lighthouse has a helipad, although some with no suitable surface base have a pad less than 30 feet (9 metres) in diameter constructed above the lantern. Entry to the lighthouse is via trapdoor in overhead pads. Helidecks are fitted to the lightvessels.

Although this type of operation normally calls for a small helicopter because of the limitations of the landing sites, there is also a strong case for twin-engine safety, so the number of helicopters that can meet both requirements is limited.

(H) Harbour pilot ferrying

The task of getting a seapilot aboard an incoming ship or getting him off an outgoing vessel has always been fraught with risk and delay due to the

A Bo. 105 of Management Aviation servicing Bishop Rock in the Atlantic

Putting a harbour pilot on board a ship off the German coast

vagaries of weather. The use of the helicopter for such operations has removed most of the risk of transferring from a small pilot boat to a ship's side ladder in running seas, and has reduced delays due to inclement weather, but above all it has brought speed to what was a time consuming affair.

The major ports of the world operate the service day and night as long as the vessel or its lights are visible from the helicopter from a minimum distance of one half-mile (800 m) at 150 ft (45 m) above sea level, at which height the helicopter must be clear of clouds. This necessitates a twin-engine helicopter certificated for instrument flight and with sophisticated navigation equipment.

There are, however, weather limits particularly of wind. When the wind velocity is above 55 knots (102 km/h), the resultant air turbulence and sea swell are usually such that the combination of movement of both the ship and the helicopter makes the operation dangerous.

Many ships do not have the space for a helideck, so the seapilot has to be lowered or picked up by a winch fitted to the helicopter. This is an electrically actuated hydraulic hoist sited externally on the side of the helicopter beside one of the entrance doors, which must be of the sliding type or be removed to give free unobstructed access.

The recommended dimensions and procedures for use of ship helidecks and winching areas are given in a document titled *Guide to Helicopter/Ship Operations* produced by the International Chamber of Shipping in conjunction with the British Helicopter Advisory Board, and now regarded world-wide as the authoritative guide on the subject.

(J) Ship resupply

The advent of the supertanker brought a new dimension into shipping. These mammoths of the sea, fully automated and with a mini-crew, have such colossal draught that only deep harbours are open to them, and docking fees are enormous. It is therefore both a physical necessity and economic sound common sense to keep such ships constantly in the open sea between departure point and destination, and this is achieved by underway resupply of cargo, mail and personnel.

One of the densest ship traffic routes in the world is off South Africa's Cape of Good Hope, where a tanker is to be seen virtually every hour. This is the key route from the oil fields of the Middle East to the consumer customers in the West. Even the Suez Canal does not affect tanker traffic much because these goliaths are just too large for passage through such restricted waterways.

Resupply off the Cape of Good Hope is perhaps the best example of use of the helicopter for this purpose. Court Helicopters provide a round-the-clock service every day of the year, operating from a helipad in the dock area to rendezvous with the ships normally 12 miles (19 km) offshore, but this distance is flexible up to about 100 miles (160 km) to ensure that no deviation of course or reduction in ship speed is necessary.

Vessels normally cable their estimated time of arrival (ETA) and provision requirements to their shore agents forty-eight hours and twelve hours prior to arrival at the rendezvous point. Cargoes are delivered to the helicopter hangar two hours prior to intended departure time. Apart from normal provisions, specialised items such as generators can be taken provided they do not weigh more than 3000 lb (1500 kg). Many stores items are carried in large external nets slung underneath the helicopter.

One hour before arrival at the rendezvous point, the ship will call the shore radio station, confirming its ETA. Fifteen minutes before arrival at the rendezvous a final confirmation is given and then the helicopter takes off. Once airborne the helicopter establishes VHF radio contact with the ship, and receives details of position, course, relative wind speed, swell, weather and visibility. Vessels will normally be asked to transmit a radio signal for homing purposes, and at night or in marginal weather conditions a locked key continuous transmission will be requested. The same operating limits are observed as in harbour pilot ferrying, and so an IFR certificated twin-engine helicopter is generally used, carrying a single-engine payload to enable safe fly-away from the ship in the event of engine failure. Payload will of course vary with range and wind speed but should be about 2500 to 3000 lb (1100–1700 kg).

Normally the helicopter lands on the ship, but if the vessel is rolling more

Supplying a tanker at sea by helicopter

than five degrees or pitching more than ten degrees or has no helideck, the service is carried out in the hover position at a height of 30 to 50 feet (9–15 m) over the chosen deck area.

The changing on passage of tanker crews by helicopter is normal practice, but also when a tanker is due to dock for maintenance, a small team of key technicians can be flown aboard some three days before the actual docking to make preparations, which reduce time in dock considerably. Underway repairs to avoid docking can also be made by flying specialists on board and picking them up some eighteen hours later.

Ship resupply is big business for the helicopter operator as can be seen by the fact that Court Helicopters has in three years carried over 17 000 tons (or metric tonnes) of supplies, ferried some 22 000 passengers, and has serviced 147 different shipping companies, and all this with an admirable record of both regularity and safety.

(K) Geophysical survey

Most of the mineral wealth of the world lies in hostile or inaccessible terrain, so its discovery has always presented a severe challenge to man. The arrival of the helicopter on the scene did not in itself radically change the situation but its coincidence with modern technological detection devices revolutionised the whole business when the two tools were welded together.

The early relatively unsophisticated detection devices were usually slung well below the helicopter and gave reaction readings on a measuring recorder carried in the cockpit. Such equipment has been refined, and as an example of the new degree of sophistication Geo Metrics, a Californian firm, has

Survey work by a Jet Ranger for the Trans-Alaska gas pipeline

fitted a turn-key radiometric survey platform just below the underbelly of a single-engine helicopter between the landing skid legs. This device is used for high resolution uranium exploration, and has 2048 crystal detectors of one cubic inch (16.39 cm^3) carried in exterior racks. Inside the cabin is a multi-channel gamma-ray spectrometer, detector interface, and airborne magnetometer. In addition there are digital and analogue data acquisition systems carried. Similar type devices are being evolved for many types of minerals.

Approximately 70% of the earth's sedimentary basins, the locations where anomalies indicating oil deposits are most likely to be found, remain unexplored. Many of these basins are in remote or inaccessible areas, which are difficult to explore by ground or marine surveys. Gravity and magnetic methods of survey provide excellent information on the general geological structures that govern the emplacement of a wide range of minerals and the traps for hydrocarbons. Magnetometers and gravity meters are used extensively for heavy metal exploration such as iron and copper. The general structure information obtained can be useful in ground water studies, land use planning, and for broad economic review.

Gravimetric measurement techniques have been in use for geophysical exploration since the early 1920s, but a practical airborne gravity system is a fairly recent achievement and much of the credit for this goes to the Geoscience Division of Carson Helicopters based in Pennsylvania. They have produced the world's only continuous profiling gravity system, which can record 3000 to 10000 line-miles (5000–16000 line-kilometres) of gravity data a month in any terrain. This system is flown internally in a Sikorsky S–61 with an advanced flight stabilisation system. Line-mile costs with the helicopter are about the same as those with ground surveys, but of course the helicopter can conduct surveys where no other vehicle can do so, and the benefits to petroleum and mining exploration are significant.

A somewhat unusual departure from the mineral scene is the measurement of ice thickness. This is done by an airborne surveying radar that uses spatial distribution of scattered waves to determine distance. Mounted between the landing skid legs of a helicopter it can measure the thickness of ice up to four metres, about the maximum thickness that powerful icebreakers are capable of penetrating. Its practical use is therefore to pick out the safest and easiest routes for icebreakers and pipelines.

Tied in with geophysical survey is topographic survey, where again the helicopter is mated with modern technology to produce a precision measuring system that is labour saving, especially in difficult and dangerous terrain. Although much can be done by aerial photography there are areas where higher precision work is required. The Hydro-Quebec Engineering Department have devised a laser system to give a vertical reference point

A Jet Ranger measuring ice thickness by airborne surveying radar

over which the helicopter hovers at a known altitude while surveyors take measurements from the ground. The laser has the property of maintaining a narrow beam diameter, which is reflected toward the pilot through a grid of optical elements mounted in front of the helicopter and thus expanded to a diameter of 2 feet (60 cm) so there is no risk to the pilot's eyes. The pilot can only see the shining light as long as the helicopter is directly over the laser. This is a simple piloting exercise which gives a high accuracy result.

Topographical survey by helicopter has proved particularly cost effective for power line and pylon location, and for highway survey especially over mountainous or wooded terrain.

Man's endless search for minerals and oil deposits, for hydro-electric power and other energy sources, and the recovery of such resources will require survey work for as far ahead as one can see, and so will supply the helicopter operator with a major area of potential revenue.

(L) Whaling

Although the use of the helicopter for spotting whales is almost extinct, largely because the mighty mammals themselves are in danger of extinction, the operation rates an honourable mention because apart from rescue work it did more initially to advertise the ability of the helicopter to operate under difficult environmental conditions, and it was one of the earliest commercial ventures that exploited the helicopter successfully.

Whaling has always been a rugged life demanding courage, and so it was for the helicopter pilots embarked on these voyages into arctic seas. They flew single-engine helicopters from a small helideck in conditions of low temperatures, and sudden weather changes, with very unreliable meteorological information, minimal navigation aids, and no diversion airfields except an ice floe or some barren, frozen coast. There was the ever present danger of a 'white-out', when wind-blown snow made the world outside the cockpit opaque.

The demands on pilot skill were high, but these pioneers brought helicoptering a wealth of experience on shipboard and arctic operations that paid great future dividends.

The list of aerial work is constantly expanding as the versatility of the helicopter is realised and exploited in an incredible variety of tasks. Some of these are now briefly commented on:

(a) *Fish shoal detection:* The sea is one of the major sources of food for the world's steadily expanding population. Beyond the coastal areas, where fishing is barely worthwhile, there are large and still unexploited oceanic zones which can provide ample quantities of food in the near future, provided new types of ship design and improved methods of fish catching are devised. Any new catching method will require a helicopter to locate shoals of fish by lowering an echo sounder into the sea by a reeling device and getting a readout on an image screen in the cockpit.

Meanwhile the simple small helicopter and crew combination are still used to spot larger fish such as tuna, rather in the style of the whalers but in a more congenial environment.

(b) *Fish stocking:* Fish breeding under controlled conditions is normally carried out well away from the environment into which the developing fish will eventually be released to struggle to maturity. The transfer may be over distances where time and motion take a heavy toll of the densely stocked 'youngsters'. Transfer by helicopter can reduce the death rate enormously, and this has proved particularly so in stocking some 250 mountain lakes with trout fingerlings in New York State.

(c) *Shellfishing:* Off the Oregon coast in western U.S.A., helicopters are setting and retrieving special crab pots of stainless steel mesh measuring 78 inches (198 cm) in diameter and 12 inches (30.5 cm) deep. Suspended from a three-sided nylon rope sling equipped with brightly coloured buoys, the pots are attached to the helicopter's cargo hook and flown from a quarter to a half-mile (400–800 m) offshore and lowered into eight to ten fathoms (15 to 18 m) of water. The buoys not only mark the location of the pots but suspend the line to facilitate retrieval.

One pilot can lay or retrieve 60 pots, which in Oregon averaged 27.5 crabs per pot. A four-hour helicopter harvest averages four times as much as a six-hour crab boat harvest. Helicopter regularity of operation is also higher and the helicopter's ability to retrieve pots quickly when a storm approaches avoids loss of equipment. The helicopter can also place pots near reefs and shoals where boats cannot safely operate.

This type of operation is equally applicable to lobstering and craying.

(d) *Wildlife protection:* Throughout the world wildlife experts keep track of animals, determine their population, food, and living habits, and chart their migration routes. In this work the helicopter is playing an invaluable part.

One of the main problems facing wardens who patrol game reserves in Africa is the illegal slaughter of wildlife by poachers, who are lured by the large sums of money being paid for rhinoceros horns and elephant ivory. The heavy toll on the rhinoceros in particular is such that the animal is threatened with extinction. The helicopter on patrol acts as a deterrent to poachers; it can also pursue and catch active poachers. Airborne game wardens can find wounded animals, tranquilise them with darts fired from the air, and land and treat them.

Another fascinating facet of wildlife protection is the tagging of polar bears, brown bears, moose and caribou in the Arctic. The tranquiliser darts fired by the game biologists have a range of only 40 yards (37 m), so the helicopter has to fly closer than that to ensure a hit. After hitting the animal, the helicopter follows until it falls unconscious, then a landing has to be made to tag, examine and weigh it.

Seal tagging is in some ways the most demanding on helicopter pilot skill.

As soon as the helicopter approaches the seals on the beaches they make for the sea, so the pilot has to make a run-on landing to intercept the animal and the tagger has to leap out and pounce on the seal as the helicopter slithers to a halt.

(e) *Ranching:* In U.S.A. and South America cattle ranchers round up the beasts twice a year – in spring when the calves are brought in for branding, and in the autumn when the cattle are gathered for delivery to market. The helicopter has proved a useful and effective cowboy in herding the cattle by staying behind them, swinging back and forth and just keeping them moving in the desired direction. In addition the machine earns its keep by inspecting fences, water holes, pumps, windmills, pipelines, and carrying out general transport duties on the extensive ranches to be found in the Americas.

(f) *Local authority duties:* The City of New York has used helicopters to trace home owners who had not registered swimming pools built in their backyards. An English local council has made a helicopter survey of possible rubbish tip sites. Idaho Transportation Department used helicopters to pick up abandoned cars, often in otherwise inaccessible places, and transport

Ridding the landscape of abandoned cars

them to a breaker's yard, thus ridding the landscape of these eyesores.

(g) *Customs surveillance:* Maritime countries always have the problem of ensuring that their coastline is not penetrated by smugglers from the seaboard side or the land side using small craft particularly in areas characterised by inlets, coves, and river estuaries.

Such a coastline typifies the French Mediterranean, and so for the past twenty years the French customs has employed two helicopters to patrol this rugged area. At sea their principal role is in identification of ships in the five mile zone (8 km zone), and when a suspect boat is located the helicopter alerts the nearest coastguard patrol torpedo boat. Inland they patrol the approaches to the possible coastal anchorages, and carry out supervision and control of secondary airports. About 800 hours per year is flown on each helicopter.

An Alouette of French customs on the Mediterranean coast

(h) *Narcotics eradication:* Approximately six tonnes of pure heroin are imported into the U.S.A. annually, of which four tonnes come from Mexico and two tonnes from South East Asia. Two-thirds of all the heroin smuggled into the U.S.A. is produced in a 30 000 square mile (77 700 km²) area of the Sierra Madre in north-west Mexico, where the opium poppy fields are cultivated by peasants. Marijuana is also raised in the same area, but mostly further south.

In an attempt to remove these social evils, the Mexican Attorney General's Office employs helicopters both to seek out and destroy the dreaded plants that yield the drugs. This is no easy task, for the peasants who grow the plants illegally do so in the most remote and rugged areas to avoid detection. The fields are small and often are cut into the face of cliffs or steep hillsides, or tucked away under a protective mountain overhang or under trees along the edge of a river. Moreover, because of the handsome profits involved, the growers are not against shooting at the prying helicopters or stringing snag wires deliberately across canyons.

The system used in Mexico is to make a sector reconnaissance with multi-spectral photographic equipment, which records multiple images through special filters that make poppy and marijuana fields stand out in photos, although they would be invisible to the human eye from high altitudes. On the basis of this photographic evidence a visual reconnaissance is made by the helicopters, who pinpoint the offending fields on a map. A temporary forward base is then set up near the target fields, and helicopters bring in fuel, herbicides and personnel. The spraying helicopters then start on the fields, while other helicopters with armed men aboard fly cover in case of running into ground gunfire. Next day a further reconnaissance is made over the fields to check that the herbicide has taken effect.

In 1977 the Mexican helicopters destroyed 27 000 poppy fields and 18 000 marijuana fields, each averaging about five acres (two hectares) in size, but the greedy peasants will continue to plant as long as the profits remain attractive.

(j) *Roadside repair:* A Californian garage owner has shown the way to a new use for small helicopters. He covers a seventy mile (110 km) radius of highways criss-crossing the state in his area, answering breakdown calls on trucks carrying 'hot cargoes' – goods that have to be at a certain point at a specific time, whatever the cost. Since a high percentage of such breakdowns is caused by electrical trouble, no heavy equipment is required to be carried in the helicopter. Besides trucks, the repair service is extended to construction, farm and mining equipment, where the cost of delay due to breakdown can be expensive.

A Bell 47 brings the flying mechanic to the aid of a disabled truck

(k) *Trucking monitoring:* A Quebec trucking company that specialises in the transportation of liquid and dry bulk commodities, many of them dangerous, such as explosives, phosphorus, sulphuric acid, propane and chlorine, employs a helicopter for traffic surveys and checking routes through congested areas.

The company is also able to check the whereabouts of trucks, since each truck carries a roof number, and it can monitor whether they are on schedule, as well as fly mechanics and spares to them in event of breakdown. Perhaps most important of all, the company can fly in expert advice in the event of an accident involving dangerous cargo.

(l) *Anti-pollution:* The oceans of the world have always been a dumping ground for rubbish of all descriptions, and because the sea has an immense self-purifying capacity it has not suffered in the past. New dangers now threaten a state of marine imbalance, as hydrocarbons from oil discharged deliberately or accidentally from giant tankers are added to those of industrial waste, sewage, and urban waste water to destroy marine animal and vegetable life.

The accidental oil discharge is the pollution area where the helicopter has been used to spread dispersant chemicals with great effectiveness, because the oil slicks can be seen easily from the air and the dispersant released, more efficiently in consequence. Furthermore the rotor down wash stirs up the water's surface and greatly facilitates emulsifying of the dispersant with the oil. The method of dispersal used by the helicopter is similar to the water douse bucket used in fighting forest fires. Above all the helicopter provides incomparable rapidity of intervention.

(m) *Archaeological surveying:* The helicopter has proved a boon to the archaeologist in research of hidden vestiges of former civilisations, which lie buried underground. To the slow-flying helicopter these treasures of the past are revealed by observation of differences in ground colouration, micro-reliefs underlined by cast shadows, and unusual changes in the growth pattern of vegetation.

Often the aerial discoveries are only made during exceptional natural phenomena, dry spells, floods, fires, etc. The changed circumstances reveal to the human eye observing from above, what had lain invisible for generations.

The helicopter is also ideal for underwater searches to a depth of about fifty feet (fifteen metres) according to the clarity of the water. The coastal strip that can be surveyed in this way varies from a few metres to several kilometres (few yards to several thousands of yards) depending on pollution and slope of the seabed.

(n) *Bank data transportation (U.S.A.):* Banking is providing a fast growing application of the helicopter. A cheque or draft on another bank deposited in a branch bank is floating, i.e. not earning interest, until it is cleared by the bank of origin. This delay can cost large banks very large sums of money, but can be avoided by using a helicopter for pick-ups.

The helicopter makes the rounds of the branch banks and lands on their rooftop helipads to pick up bags of documents, or if no such helipad is available it uses an automatic rig whereby the bag with a ring handle is placed on top of a pole and the helicopter hovers over the pole and retrieves the bag by use of a hand-held hook placed through the ring handle.

Some of these operations are pool operations requiring the use of different coloured bags for identification of the banks involved; others are run by individual banks. Some banks own their helicopters outright, others charter them.

Citizens and Southern National Bank of Atlanta began helicopter pick-ups in 1966 and ten years later had three Jet Rangers making a total of 134 pick-ups each day, totalling some 3300 flying hours a year.

(o) *Property selection:* The helicopter has proved a useful sales tool for real estate dealers who take clients to view sites from the air and give them a hitherto unobtainable perspective. This method has been particularly successful in relation to industrial sites, sports areas and farmland.

(p) *Chimney sweeping:* This must just about be the ultimate in the exploitation of the helicopter's versatility, but Mr Bent Mikelsen in Denmark has been using a small Hughes 300 to perch him on rooftops beside the chimney stack he is about to sweep. It is claimed that this method allows Mr Mikelsen to carry out in one day the work that formerly took two weeks.

(q) *Fallout dispersal:* With the eruption of Mount St Helens in Washington state, U.S.A. in 1980, volcanic ash fell over a wide area. One severely affected region was Yakima Valley, where orchards of some 47000 acres of apples, 6000 acres of cherries, 12000 acres of pears, and 3000 acres of peaches were blossoming. Helicopters were used to fly at slow speed just above the fruit trees to free them from their heavy coating of ash by rotor downwash effect, as the ash would otherwise intercept insecticide chemicals later applied and thus threaten crop health. This was so successful that the system was applied to power lines and transformers, whose performance was suffering from the ash, whose weight was also straining the lighter lines and whose sulphuric content could have corrosive effects.

There seems to be no limit to the tasks the helicopter may fulfil, and it only remains for the ingenuity of man to exploit this remarkable tool to the full.

Chapter 6

The flying crane

The lifting capability of a helicopter depends on its power/weight ratio, which in general increases with the size of the helicopter. Most civil helicopters are not designed with large internal cargo stowage, so if the maximum lifting capacity is to be realised it means slinging the load externally under the aircraft on a cargo hook on the end of a line attached to the underbelly near the centre of gravity of the helicopter.

A Sikorsky Skycrane lifts a cooling unit into position on a rooftop

Heavy lift developed as wider markets were sought for the early helicopters. Gradually it was realised that the vertical lift capacity of the helicopter makes it an excellant crane vehicle and indeed often the only practical solution for applications where limited access, very rough terrain or sheer height prevent the use of mobile cranage.

The Skycrane

At first there were no specialist heavy lift helicopters, because the market was limited and the capital investment required for such a machine was enormous. Again the military application paved the way for such a specialised requirement and the Sikorsky Skycrane was born. Actually it began as a private venture, the brainchild of the great Igor Sikorsky, and cost two million dollars to build. Its potential might never have been fully realised if the Vietnamese War had not come along to allow it to carry out such tasks as landing 224 tons (203 metric tonnes) of equipment from the Australian aircraft-carrier 'Sydney' in four-and-a-quarter hours. ʼ

The S–64 Skycrane is such a remarkable concept that it deserves some detailed description. It is twin turbine-powered, and first flew on 9 May 1962. It is designed to carry up to ten tons of payload externally. In addition to the normal pilot seating it has a rear-facing pilot's seat, so that he can take

The Skycrane transports a prefabricated house

over and position the cargo with extreme precision. It is a very large helicopter with a 72 ft (22 m) diameter rotor, an overall length of 88 ft 6 in (27 m) and a height of 18 ft 7 in (5.5 m), and it has a ground clearance of 9 ft 4 in (2.8 m). Maximum gross weight is 42 000 lb (19 000 kg), and its twin engines develop 9000 horsepower (6700 kw).

On the North Slope of Alaska two S–64 helicopters transported 11 915 tons (12 105 tonnes) of equipment and supplies over impassable tundra during a three month operation, averaging 150 flight hours per month with a 95% availability rate.

Probably the most spectacular task ever undertaken by the Skycrane was the placing of the 335 foot (102 m) antenna on top of the CN Tower in Toronto, the world's highest free-standing building, in March 1975. The

A Skycrane of Erickson Air Crane Co. placing the antenna section on top of the CN Tower in Toronto

antenna was lifted up in thirty-nine sections at a cost of 7000 dollars a day while the job lasted. The price may seem high, for the total flight time involved in each lift is small – literally from the bottom of the tower to the top – but it is a relatively low cost when compared with the alternative method. In fact the structural contractor on the tower project estimated that the use of the Skycrane cut construction costs by 80%.

Relative cost is what heavy lift is all about. For example an S–64E delivered 52 tons (53 metric tonnes) of heavy equipment to a Gulf of Mexico oil rig some 25 miles (40 km) offshore, making eleven round trips in 2½ hours of flying time. By conventional barge movement the operation would have taken some 24 hours.

The S–64 is not the heaviest helicopter lifter in the world, as the Russian Mi–V.12 has lifted 44½ tons (45 metric tonnes), but it is not in production. The heaviest production civil helicopter lifter is the Boeing-Vertol Chinook, which can lift 28 000 lb (12 700 kg) on the centre hook. This helicopter also has a twin hook layout, with a loading strength of 16 000 lb (7250 kg) on each hook.

Slingload aerodynamics

In conducting heavy lift operations the first consideration is choice of route, which must allow for the possibility of the cargo having to be jettisoned in emergency. Only twin-engine helicopters should be used in built-up areas. If

A military Chinook lifting a tank

A Boeing-Vertol Chinook carrying three underslung portable fuel containers

the external load has a significant flat plate area the resultant drag will cause an increase in fuel consumption and decrease in cruise speed, so range will suffer.

Generally, rectangular, cylindrical or conical cargoes will tend to streamline in flight, so that the longitudinal axis of the load parallels that of the aircraft. However, all external loads, regardless of shape, exhibit aerodynamic lifting properties in a fast-moving, free airstream.

The external load is normally carried in webbed collars, nylons slings or cargo nets, which in turn are connected to the cargo hook. There must be at least two quick-release devices in the cargo hook winch system, one to be installed on one of the pilot's primary controls and the other to be a manually activated mechanical control accessible to the crew. The Chinook has five methods of opening the cargo hook.

The behaviour or reaction of an external load in flight is of primary importance to the pilot. The high density load (large mass per unit of volume) is the most stable and ordinarily presents no problems. The low density load (small mass per unit of volume) can be unstable in flight so is always a potential hazard. Aerodynamic loads such as crashed aircraft can be the most dangerous of all unless very carefully rigged to cancel lift-creating properties. Often such loads require use of a stabilising drogue similar to a sea anchor.

A swaying or swinging load can give the helicopter pilot an unpleasant ride, and it can easily result in him getting the controls out of phase with the periodicity of the swing and so aggravate the condition. The best way of controlling this situation is to slow down the helicopter.

The ground crew play an important part in external load operations, and a set of ground signals must be agreed with the marshaller, even if he is using radio instructions under normal circumstances. All ground crew should wear industrial safety goggles to avoid eye injury from downwash disturbance effects, while loaders must wear heavy gloves as protection against static electricity. Since a heavy lift helicopter can generate 15000 volts in its electrostatic envelope, it is desirable to ground the static by using a shepherd's crook type device to touch the airframe and load at the same time before hook-up or off-loading. However, if potentially explosive cargoes are permitted to be carried externally, earthing through the cargo itself should be avoided.

Construction heavy lift

The main benefactor from the heavy lift helicopter has been the construction industry. Small single piston-engine Hiller 12Es each lifting 800 lb (350 kg) of concrete mix were used in Hong Kong to dash up and down to the top of a hill in this crowded settlement where a high-rise hotel was being built. At the other end of the scale S–64s were used in Holland to lift massive 10-ton (10.2-tonne) loads of concrete from land to be dropped into the sea to form a dyke.

A Jet Ranger hooking up a load atop a Norwegian mountain

Setting a cable car pylon in position

Certain areas of construction work such as lifting cooling generators to rooftop sites, setting up power line poles, erecting electric grid pylons, laying pipelines, and building ski-lifts are particularly suited to the heavy lift helicopter.

The most demanding heavy lift task being regularly undertaken is that by Erickson Air Crane in the mid-west of the U.S.A., where they have been erecting steel transmission towers for 500-kV power lines. Their S–64E Skycranes pick up 18000 lb (8000 kg) sections and place them one atop the other without the necessity of men being on the tower. The company has designed its own guide system using a spreader bar which keeps the tower section from turning in flight, and allows the pilot in the rear facing cockpit to slip the section's four legs direct into the special reusable guides bolted to the top of the standing tower section. The spreader bar stabilises the tower so that the pilot actually has to turn the helicopter to turn the tower.

Hand in hand with power line pole and tower erection goes the stringing of the conductor, which is a metal cable carrying the current. The helicopter

An impression of the Commercial Chinook placing the massive top section of a steel transmission tower in position

pulls the $^3/_8$ inch (9.5 mm) steel cable sideways on a special frame, and by use of a special device on each tower can thread the cable through this and so on to the next.

Special tasks

A very unusual heavy lift job in Ecuador involved transporting a 1¼ inch (32 mm) wire cable 2500 ft (750 m) long and weighing 7125 lb (3230 kg) over a distance of 28 miles (45 km) over dense jungle terrain. The special construction of the cable did not allow it to be cut or divided, so it had to be moved in one piece.

No single helicopter with sufficient lift capability was available in the area, so the wire was arranged in two spools with the weight distributed according to the lift capability of the two different types of helicopter available, and with a 200 ft (60 m) length of cable between them. In case the external load on one helicopter was lost in flight for any reason, an electrical system was installed in both aircraft which would automatically release the load on either helicopter in the event that the load was lost on the other.

A likely growth area of heavy lift operations is in unloading ships in constricted ports. Many developing nations with a rapidly expanding economy find that economy being slowly strangled by the inadequacy of their main ports to deal with the mass inflow of shipping bringing the materials and equipment so badly needed by the country. Such a ship jam occurred in the Saudi Arabian port of Jeddah, where upwards of 200 freighters queued up to unload. At best the turnaround time for a ship was about forty days and some ships were having to wait up to six months for their turn to discharge their cargo. The consequent demurrage charges were colossal and the government's five-year development plan was being jeopardised by shortages of critically needed goods, two-thirds of which flow through Jeddah.

In this desperate situation the Saudi government placed a contract with Carson Helicopters of Pennsylvania, U.S.A. for the use of eight S–58T twin-turbine helicopters for the period of one year to offload cement from the jammed up ships. In that time Carson's helicopters unloaded twelve million 110-pound (50-kg) bags of cement in 300 000 round trips amounting to 15 000 flight hours. The helicopter operated twelve hours a day for six days a week. Each pilot flew a four hour shift with a four minute refuelling stop every hour, even the refuelling being made without shutting down in order to save time. Maintenance was performed at night, and in spite of the operating environment of heat, desert sand, cement dust, salt water, and ship's funnel gases, there were no major or mechanical failures during the year.

The helicopters were flown by a single pilot, and were fitted with a 100 ft (30 m) steel cable carrying a net for picking a 4400 lb (2000 kg) load every two to three minutes. During peak periods 3500 tons (3556 tonnes) of cement per day were offloaded – nearly double the 2000 tons (2032 tonnes) specified in the contract.

Although the Sikorsky S–58T medium lift helicopter used in this remarkable operation is basically a barely modified civil version of a military type capable of lifting 5000 lb (2250 kg) externally, it is significant that the Bell 214B 'Big Lifter', twin-turbine medium helicopter specifically developed for heavy lift and available just a year before the Jeddah saga began, has a lift capacity of 7000 lb (3175 kg) on the hook although it is a considerably smaller helicopter than the S–58T.

Aerial logging

A widespread use of helicopter heavy lift is in the logging industry. The old methods of logging were very destructive to young saplings in that the larger trees when felled had to be dragged by tractor to a handling and loading site,

A Vertol 107 plucking logs out of a timber forest

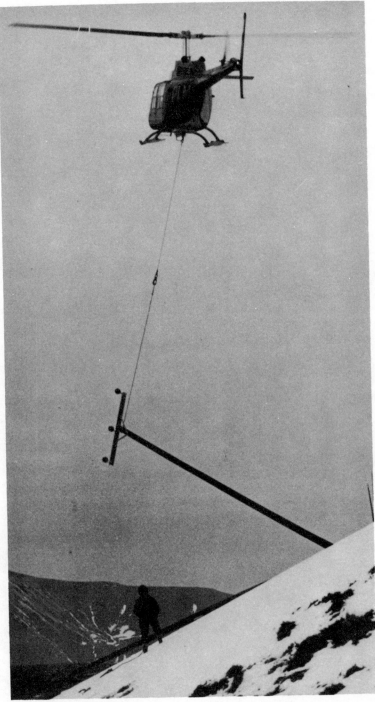

A Jet Ranger placing a ski-lift pole on Scottish mountain slope

and therefore each log acted in effect as a bulldozer on this journey, destroying everything in its path.

The helicopter makes selective logging a simple proposition. The logger fells only the trees he wants to use for lumber, then airlifts them to a central loading site, whence they are trucked directly to the sawmill. This system produces a healthier forest, allowing more space for growth, and also preserves the natural beauty of forestation. It also permits the logging of trees in areas of inaccessible terrain.

The felling of logs specifically for uplift by helicopter is very important, so that an optium load is achieved and abortive attempts avoided. All branches must be lopped off, the weight of the trunk estimated, and enough clear space made available to avoid pulling the logs up through the branches of standing trees.

Helicopter maintenance costs are considerably higher than normal in logging lifts, for maximum power is often required. Turnaround time is vital to production profits, so normally the distance from the logging area to the landing area should not exceed 1½ miles (2½ km). It is also safer to have the landing area above the logging area to prevent any risk of power settling in the approach with the load.

High lift

The construction of ski-lifts brings a new factor into heavy lift, namely altitude. The contractor starts by digging footing holes in the summer months, and then he brings in the helicopter carrying externally slung buckets of concrete, which are tipped into the holes. The towers are then flown up and attached to the concrete footings, all this at altitudes up to 8000 ft (2500 m). It is the 'hot and high' syndrome compounded by strong winds, swirling air currents, and sloping terrain, all of which add up to a real challenge to the skill of the helicopter pilot.

Odd jobs

The most fascinating aspect of heavy lift work is the incredible variety of unusual tasks that are offered to the helicopter, most of them once only types of operation. Some examples of these will best illustrate not only the unique aspect, but also the cost effectiveness of using the helicopter for the job.

In Costa Rica in 1970 floodwaters isolated the Rio Trio Project's nine banana farms from the railhead across the River Rio Chirrapo. The only way of getting the millions of pounds of rapidly maturing fruit across the river to the trains was by helicopter. In this operation time and gentle handling of the fruit were of the essence, so a special sling net was devised to hold the 84-box pallet of bananas.

By flying eleven to twelve hours per day with a 1½–2 min refuelling stop hourly, Petroleum Helicopters Inc. of Louisiana moved about 90 million pounds (40 million kg) of bananas from processing sheds to railroad in a seven-month period. With only one helicopter, a Bell 205A–1, on task it achieved an average of more than 200 hours flight time for each twenty-eight day work period. In the seven months a total of 2 287 500 boxes of fruit, each weighing 40 pounds (18 kg) were uplifted. For the first two months the haul distance was 5 miles (8 km) and thereafter 1½ miles (2½ km). Apart from a noon time inspection, maintenance was done at night or on the occasional rest day.

One of Helicopter Hire's Bell 47 Series helicopters engaged on a publicity promotion flight carrying the 3000th petrol pump for BP from Battersea to Chelmsford along the Thames

In the spring of 1970 the 8500 ton (8636 tonne) freighter 'Vaniene' loaded with 300 cars manufactured in Japan ran aground on rock some 30 miles (48 km) north of the strait leading to its port of destination, Vancouver. Normal salvage methods were unsuccessful and Okanagan Helicopters was called in to help salvage the cars not touched by water. The deck rigging and ship's cargo booms were removed, and using 100 ft (30 m) of line from a Bell 204B, a total of 131 cars were removed from holds down to three levels below the upper deck. The whole operation took two days including dismantling the obstacles on the upper deck surface.

In Pontiac, Michigan, a football stadium was to have an air-supported fabric roof fitted over it, the job being scheduled for completion by mid-August 1975. Because of construction delays associated with the installation of eighteen three inch (76 mm) diameter roof support cables, the project fell six weeks behind schedule.

By using Evergreen Helicopters' S–64 Skycrane to lift and position the 16 000 lb (7250 kg) cables on the end of its 75 ft (23 m) sling, the job was completed in a day-and-a-half, with a flight time of some eight-and-a-half hours, allowing the 10-acre (4-hectares) roof to be in service on schedule.

A new use introduced in 1977 was aerial harvesting of young trees at nursery sites. The helicopter, using a 15 foot (4.5 m) steel cable and cargo hook distributed the empty 300 lb (136 kg) collapsed pallets around the field where workers filled them with trees. In this way the helicopter could uplift over 100 000 trees in a five-hour day, while ground vehicle methods only averaged about 80 000 trees in a nine-hour day. The grower was thus able to reduce his time and labour requirements by almost one-third, but above all he could control the market by beginning harvesting much later than conventional growers. An added benefit was that helicopter-harvested trees can remain longer on the stump and thus arrive fresher.

The heavy lift future

The future for heavy lift helicopters is perhaps the brightest in the whole spectrum of helicopter operations, for the progress to be made in undeveloped countries throughout the world will inevitably require aerial cranes in terrain where roads are scarce or non-existent and natural barriers of all kinds abound.

Even in the sophisticated environment of western civilisation the heavy lift helicopter has barely got off the ground in terms of utilisation, because its lift capacity has too often been inadequate. The construction field will be its main arena, and soon modular buildings will be seen rising like stacks of children's bricks, with complete pre-fabricated storeys placed one on top of the other by aerial crane. There will be no expensive mobile cranes with huge jibs to be brought at a snail's pace through traffic jammed roads, no lengthy preparatory work rigging the equipment on site, and no damage to cultivated areas around the site. It will be a clinically clean and swift operation.

The crane pilot

In heavy lift work the skill of the pilot probably counts more than in any other kind of helicopter operation, and yet very little has been done to ease his task except in the case of the remarkable S–64 Skycrane, with its rear facing cockpit bubble, where the third pilot can take over control of the aircraft and at the same time operate the cargo winch. As part of his cockpit instrumentation he has a dynamometer, which gives him a constant reading of the load on the hook.

With this exception, the pilot always has the problem of sighting the target on which he has to place his external cargo, and he has had to lean heavily on instructions from his co-pilot, observer or ground marshaller. Evergreen Helicopters, who specialise in heavy lift, developed a bubble door containing an instrument panel with engine monitoring gauges, a torquemeter, dual tachometer, and a single-load weighing gauge. This door is fitted to the left side of the helicopter, thus displacing the pilot from the conventional first pilot's position, but the left side is the better side for looking out as the pilot is not stretching for the collective lever nor is his right arm restricted by his body in reaching the cyclic control.

Lift capacity

The range of lifting capacity of the civil helicopters in use today is:

	lb	kg
Boeing–Vertol Chinook	28000	12700
Sikorsky S–64E Skycrane	12000	5400
Sikorsky S–61	8000	3600
Aerospatiale 330J Puma	7700	3500
Bell 214 Big Lifter	7000	3200
Sikorsky S–58T	5000	2300
Bell 212	5000	2300
Sud-Aviation Lama	2500	1100
Bolkow Bo. 105	1700	800
Hiller 12 Soloy Conversion	1250	570
Bell Jet Ranger	1200	550
Hiller 12E	800	350

The Soloy Conversion of the Hiller 12 light helicopter is the replacement of the 345 h.p. (350 C.V.) piston-engine with a 400 s.h.p. (405 C.V.) turbine engine.

Chapter 7

The aerial Rolls-Royce

The executive helicopter is a comparative newcomer on the rotary-wing scene, and it really began with the advent of the turbine-engined, four passenger Bell Jet Ranger in about 1968. This was the first helicopter with an attractive shape, easy passenger access, internal comfort, reasonable noise and vibration levels, high cruise speed and the inherent reliability of the turbine engine. All this added up to a package that interested big business, which regards rapid management mobility of major importance.

Executives are highly paid individuals and companies cannot afford to have their time wasted in lengthy periods of travel, so their employers seek time-saving travel devices. Obviously the aeroplane is the mode selected for long distances, but most executives spend 85% of their time within a 200-mile (325-kilometre) world, and as the turbine helicopter normally has a better door to door time than the aeroplane over distances up to 250 miles (400 km), it comes into the reckoning as a cost-effective business tool.

Company ownerhsip

In this reckoning the capital cost of the helicoper is progressively tax deductible, together with a percentage of the operating costs, but its justification largely will depend on its utilisation. Anything under 300 flight hours per annum is making the executive helicopter a questionable luxury, and is likely to bring the evil eye of the company accountant upon it. From a cost-effective viewpoint an annual utilisation of 500 flight hours is desirable. Also coming under the scrutiny of the executives who will use it will be the question of safety. The instinct of self-preservation is highly developed in all of us, and air travel seems to sharpen it in most of us. There is also the matter of noise and vibration, for the passengers are not likely to be interested in viewing the scenic panorama from their lofty perch, but will want to talk, read or write business en-route.

These factors will have superimposed on them the question of landing site facilities both at their home base and the other places they are likely to visit as a matter of routine. After all there is not much point in investing in a helicopter if it has no more flexibility than an aeroplane.

Often the first step taken by a company interested in acquiring an executive helicopter is to lease one for six months or a year. This will provide some answers, but not all of them. Certainly it will give staff reaction to such mode of travel, and this is almost certain to be enthusiasm once the initial strangeness of first acquaintance has worn off, and is replaced by that feeling of euphoria as one speeds in a direct line from place to place over the traffic winding its laborious way below, and without the stress and frustration that is a part of road travel, and is a factor in reducing the life span of executives well below the norm.

Leasing can be on either a 'wet lease' or 'dry lease' basis. In the latter case the hull of the aircraft itself is leased, with no other services. The term 'wet lease' originated in the shipping industry and embraces the hire of certain services to the customer as well as the lease of the aircraft hull itself. Generally the wet lease package will include all insurances associated with the operation of the aircraft, provision of flight crew, licensed ground engineers, and all maintenance and spares support, but various combinations of items between the two extremes of dry and wet lease are possible.

The lease period will also reveal whether problems of landing sites exist. Throughout the western world the regulations governing the landing of helicopters at unlicensed sites vary tremendously, but gradually a common thread is beginning to run through them. In general the landowner's permission is always required, and for single-engine helicopters there must be a clear path into and out of the site for a distance of 1½ miles (2½ km). There should also be no obstructions in the clear area above a slope of 1 in 8 from the site. Beyond these basic requirements the local laws may complicate the picture to varying degrees.

However, having been broken in on a leased aircraft, the company must now get down to brass tacks if it decides to become a proud owner. First and foremost is the matter of capital expenditure. Is the choice of helicopter to be based on ceiling cost, passenger capacity, twin-engine reliability or all-weather capability? Except in the first case there is a wide range of choice available.

In general the executive field has been dominated in the 1970s by the five-seat single turbine-engine helicopter, but this is generally operated as a VFR (Visual Flight Rules) aircraft and the wind of change is blowing. Companies are now looking to IFR (Instrument Flight Rules) capability, which virtually dictates twin-engine layout. Longer range, higher speed and more capacious cabins are also being sought.

In the small 2/3-seat class, the choice is virtually limited to the Enstrom range, which are piston-engined, although a turbine version is under development. This is a smart-looking little helicopter, reasonably quiet, but strictly a two-seater if executive comfort is required.

The single turbine-engine group offers a wide choice with the vastly popular Bell Jet Ranger, its stretched seven seat cousin the Long Ranger, the five seat Westland Gazelle with its high cruise speed of 160 m.p.h. (260 km/h) and fenestron tail rotor, the six seat Aerospatiale Squirrel and the ten seat fenestron tailed Dauphin from the same stable, the latter two aircraft really belonging to the new technology classfication. Also in that classfication is the five seat Hughes 500D, because it is really a considerable

An executive Jet Ranger overflies the traffic of a major city

advance on the earlier 500s in the matter of reduced noise level, although its rear cabin still remains too claustrophobic to earn it great executive popularity.

For some years the twin-engine group was limited to the five seat Bolkow Bo. 105 which is still improving its executive image with a more capacious rear cabin. However, 1980 brought a rush of new designs on to the twin scene, and all in the new technology classification to which the German Bolkow 105 also deserves to belong with its semi-rigid rotor. The Italian eight-seat Agusta 109, the French ten-seat Dauphin 2, the American ten-seat Bell 222 with its 170 m.p.h. (270 km/h) fast cruise, and the beautiful Sikorsky S–76 Spirit have brought a new dimension to executive travel in speed, comfort, reliability, and IFR capability.

Having settled on the helicopter type, the next question is that of maintaining it. A number of alternatives may be available. The first is the obvious one of employing a specialist helicopter staff mechanic, but this is the most expensive solution, since if a single helicopter only is owned by the company then the mechanic is going to be paid for a lot of time just sitting around while the helicopter is flying.

Another alternative is to employ a pilot with the necessary technical licences to both fly and maintain the helicopter. This is not as good a solution as it may appear at first sight, for after a day's flying the pilot may be too tired to make a thorough mechanical inspection of his aircraft. Also he tends to become attuned to his helicopter as a pilot and thus accept small variations in performance of vibration, which to the full-time mechanic would be warning signs of impending trouble.

The third alternative is by far the most practical and that is to hand over the maintenance task to an independent, local maintenance facility, but that depends on there being such a facility in the operating company's area.

If the company already owns fixed-wing aircraft and maintains these with its own staff mechanics, then the simple solution is to send one of these mechanics on a specialist helicopter technical course.

The choice of pilot may seem straightforward, but experience has shown that the executive pilot needs to have certain qualities, which may not apertain in other sectors of helicopter operations. He is going to be much more closely involved with his passengers than in any other form of public transport operation, and he must appreciate that they are all likely to stand much higher in the company hierarchy than he is as company pilot, so tact and diplomacy will be necessary assets. He will also have to assess the importance and degree of urgency of each flight to his company and take this into consideration in his flight planning. He will have to have patience, for he will be doing a lot of hanging around waiting, and he will have to be a good organiser, for he will be expected to sort out all the problems that can attend air travel, such as overnight accommodation in the event of an inevitable delay. However, in return he will be well paid, with fringe benefits and a reasonably orderly and comfortable life, and there should be variety in plenty.

This is not the kind of job likely to be suitable for an ex-agricultural pilot or military gunship pilot just out of the armed forces. Ideally candidates should have previous experience of public transport operations and be instrument rated.

The pilot chosen will want to have a say in the aircraft's equipment, for although the minimum equipment standards will be laid down by the helicopter certification authority, there is still a considerable freedom of choice of product. Radio and navigation aids are of primary importance and will be duplicated as will certain primary blind flying instruments. Auto-stabilisation will either be selected for passenger comfort in the non-IFR certificated helicopter or of necessity if it is IFR certificated. Other refinements could include a flight director, and weather radar in the bigger executive helicopter types. Sound proofing will also have to be considered for passenger comfort as well as custom built fittings for the company chairman. Then there is the matter of flotation gear for overwater safety, and whether to have wheels or skids (if there is an option) to meet the manoeuvring requirements at the helipads likely to be frequented.

All-weather capability

The provision of all-weather or IFR (as it is generally referred to) capability has become a major marketing point for executive sales, since it offers increased regularity of operations, greater safety because of the twin-engine layout normally associated with the IFR requirement, and greater flexibility of operation. However, apart from the increased capital cost of a twin-engine model, the running costs of a helicopter type are increased by approximately 15% by the provision of IFR capability.

So far consideraiton has only been given to the internal equipment of the executive helicopter to allow it to fly and navigate blind, and to let-down to certain airfields equipped with compatible ground approach aids. But there is much more to it than that if full unrestricted flexibility of operation is required.

The cockpit of an IFR equipped Bo. 105

Single-pilot IFR operation is only acceptable in uncontrolled airspace, but when in controlled airspace such as airways the work load becomes so high that two pilots are required. Furthermore the company may not expect its helicopter to be always operated in and out of airfields in bad weather, so a capability will be required to allow it to land at certain designated company helipads. This will involve a reasonably inexpensive, portable, self-contained all-weather approach aid such as a microwave landing system being available on the ground, with the associated airborne equipment in the helicopter.

Full IFR capability will be seen to be an expensive facility, but basically no more expensive than in an aeroplane except for auto-stabilisation. This latter requirement gives a clue as to why helicopters have been so late in their development in entering the IFR field. Helicopters unlike aeroplanes are inherently unstable about all three axes, so whereas the normal period for an aeroplane non-instrument rated pilot to lose control on inadvertently getting into instrument flight conditions is just over two minutes this is probably less than a minute in a helicopter.

It must be remembered that even an aeroplane instrument-rated pilot could quickly get into trouble on the early helicopters, because the fuselage is pendulous under the rotor blades, which are in effect the wings of the aircraft, and the instruments tell the position of the fuselage but not what the all important position of the wings is because there is a reaction time lag between moving the cyclic control which moves the rotor and the follow-up motion of the fuselage. In modern helicopters this situation has been largely overcome by the new technology design of rotor heads, including semi-rigid and rigid rotors.

In purchasing an executive helicopter, one is inevitably led to the question: What advantages do an IFR capability give and is it cost effective? The answer is really fourfold:

(a) The IFR environment is safer than the marginal VFR one. Every helicopter pilot has had the experience of fumbling his way along with his eyes popping out of his head looking for trees, power lines, factory chimneys, rising ground, etc. in an attempt to complete his commercial or military task. It is a situation that invites accidents.

(b) IFR capability gives the pilot an escape route in marginal weather conditions. The classic example is that of crossing water, and as the cloud ceiling lowers and visibility worsens, the pilot suddenly finds himself in a goldfish bowl of murk at very low altitude, unable to distinguish the water surface. In this situation the IFR helicopter takes the way to safety, which is up and not down.

(c) The increased professionalism and pilot proficiency associated with instrument ratings produces more competent and safer pilots.

(d) IFR capability allows a considerably higher utilisation of the helicopter and therefore makes a more cost-effective aircraft.

The association of the twin-engine layout with full helicopter IFR capability is based on the assumption that the aircraft will have unrestricted flight over congested areas of habitation. Single-engine helicopters can be IFR certificated, but they will normally only be allowed to follow certain routes, such as along a river, through built-up areas, so that in the event of engine failure they have a reasonable chance of making an autorotative landing without injury to property or a third party on the ground.

The IFR helicopter has posed a problem to air traffic control authorities in the integration of fixed-wing and rotary-wing traffic. Different operating height bands, speeds, turning circles, angles of approach and climb all call for revised ATC methods. There is no point in feeding helicopters into the standard aerodrome pattern, thus failing to recognise their special flight characteristics and taking up a slot that could be occupied by a giant airliner. These problems are in their infancy, but already there are some 2000 executive helicopters in the U.S.A. so the answers are becoming a matter of urgency.

Corporate helipads

Of course executive helicopters should not need to use aerodromes too often except to link up their passengers with main airlines, but the most frequent destinations for such helicopters will be helipads at factory and office headquarters and urban heliports.

The acquisition of a corporate helipad, whether at ground level or on a rooftop will often be more of a public relations exercise than a legal problem. No company can disregard its public image, and goodwill is a valuable commodity in that respect. The local populace around a helipad will have to be reassured about safety, noise, hours of operation, and validity of the requirement to have a helicopter.

A lot can be done to win the co-operation of the public by offering the services of the helicopter in a community emergency role. This does not mean that the false impression should be given of a twenty-four-hour availability emergency service, but that an emergency call from an authoritative source such as the police, fire chief, or hospital chief medical officer will be answered on an ad hoc basis as and when possible.

The sensible company user of a helicopter will generally be well advised to keep a low publicity profile, and not offer the helicopter as a target either for the public, the media or the shareholders, all of whom will tend to regard the aircraft as a privilege vehicle until its value is more widely understood and accepted in this specialised role.

Cost effectiveness

Cost effectiveness can best be illustrated by a practical example. In 1977 the huge American mid-western AMAX Coal Company bought an IFR Gazelle helicopter, which operates over a three state area connecting the corporate headquarters in Indianapolis with division offices in Illinois and Indiana as well as with ten mine sites and two port facilities scattered through these two states and Kentucky. The most distant mine site is 215 miles (345 km) from Indianopolis, and the helicopter will often do a six-hour stint involving up to ten take-offs and landings. In its first year AMAX's Gazelle logged 650 flight hours, of which 10% to 15% were actual instrument flight, although an IFR flight plan is generally filed for every flight.

This company, the third largest producer of coal in the U.S.A., is convinced that their executive helicopter has improved the management efficiency to a considerable degree, by more frequent face-to-face contact with the mines personnel, and the new perspective that has been gained from aerial surveys of their facilities. In short in the company's estimation their helicopter is eminently cost-effective.

A convincing public demonstration of the cost effectiveness of the executive helicopter was given on the occasion of the National Business Aviation Association Convention in 1979. On 27 September at 1.55 p.m., two groups of six people left the Hyatt Regency Hotel in Knoxville, Tennessee – one group to travel in a Sikorsky S–76 Spirit helicopter and the other in a Rockwell Sabreliner executive twin jet aeroplane. Fifty-nine minutes later the Spirit arrived at the temporary heliport in the parking lot of the World Congress Center in Atlanta, Georgia, and were in the convention hall in a total elapsed time of 1 hour 10 min, while the Sabreliner group took 1 hour 59 min to achieve the same objective.

The helicopter used less than half the fuel used by the aeroplane, and the cost per mile for the aeroplane was almost double that for the helicopter. This is a very impressive demonstration, but the key to the helicopter's success was the availability of two convenient helipads.

An interesting example of using the best of both worlds is the case of Mr Gerald Tobias, President of the Sikorsky Aircraft Company, who together with his wife and marketing director took off in a Sikorsky S–76 at 9 a.m. on 5 September 1980 from the rooftop helipad of the 220 ft high International Press Centre in the City of London and flew to London Airport in 8 minutes, boarded the supersonic jetliner Concorde for New York, where another S–76 was waiting to transport the party to Wall Street Heliport in a total elapsed time of 4 hours 26 min, thus arriving in downtown New York over half-an-hour before they left the centre of London, by local time comparisons.

Chapter 8

The helicopter in public service

There is widespread impression that helicopters only serve the public in the Search and Rescue (SAR) role, but that view probably stems from the publicity given to SAR incidents by the news media. However, there are many other areas of activity in which the helicopter serves the public in its unique fashion, and these are worth examining to get a true appreciation of the value of rotary-wing aircraft to the ordinary citizen, who is often too ready to oppose civil helicopter operations on the grounds of social unacceptability.

(A) Law enforcement

The first use of the helicopter by police was in New York in 1947, and today in 1980 every state in the U.S.A. uses helicopters in police work, embracing a total of some 1500 aircraft. This has spread to many countries in the world as the value of this modern crime fighter is revealed in so many diverse phases.

At first police air observers had only the human eye aided by powerful binoculars to provide their surveillance, but the random patrolling over a city of a helicopter marked POLICE is a powerful deterrent against crimes such as bank robberies. The actual act of holding up a bank is relatively easy compared to the getaway, which must be planned so that the traffic is not too heavy to impede the getaway vehicle on its way to the inevitable change-over vehicle. This procedure is normally highly successful, but it is rendered totally ineffective by helicopter surveillance. This illustrates the main advantage of the law enforcement helicopter – it reduces response time.

Visual observation still remains the primary method of crime detection by helicopter, and from the normal patrolling height of 500 to 700 ft (150 to 215 m), out of gunfire range, a tremendous area can be scanned. Such observation is particularly effective over large, difficult areas of terrain like railway yards, beaches, and parks, which can be checked over in minutes, whereas a foot patrol would take a lengthy time. In fact a police observer can see six times more from the air than can be seen from the ground and he can also see an object on the ground ten times longer than an officer moving at normal patrol car speed.

Aerial observation has been used very successfully against robberies, burglaries drug trafficking, mugging, and car thefts. Kansas City's use of

Removable rescue winch in position on British Airways S–61N

police helicopters caused a decline of 40% in these crimes in a year, and 175 stolen cars were recovered in two years.

Police helicopters are also very useful for traffic and crowd control, fire spotting, searching for missing persons or escaped prisoners, and baulking suicide attempts. However, the main uses will depend on the area environment and the crime pattern for that area.

Communications play a vital role in the efficiency of the police helicopter, and it must have communication with headquarters, patrol cars, and street officers. The helicopter will seldom attempt an arrest, but provides support to the ground forces. It is thus a great psychological boost to street officers in troublesome situations.

Another use the helicopter can be put to is escort duty for VIPs and bullion consignments using road transport. In such security situations the aerial policeman has a great deterent value, so much so that some cities are now encouraging the marking of buildings, vans, taxis and buses with rooftop identification numbers.

An Enstrom F28A on Metropolitan Police duty over London

The choice of helicopter for police duties is often dictated by cost, and so small two-seat machines are widely used, but bigger machines are now used to complement the smaller ones in the larger police fleets such as that in Los Angeles, which has five Bell 47s and fifteen Jet Rangers, the latter being used for rescue missions and to carry additional equipment. Virtually all police helicopters in use up to 1980 have been of the single-engine type.

There is a growing school of thought that all urban police flights should only be carried out in twin-engine helicopters, and the London Metropolitan Police has made the transition from singles to twins for safety reasons in the main.

There are also two schools of thought about the composition of crews. Some forces believe that ex-military professional helicopter pilots with some basic training in police methods should be used together with a trained police observer, while others advocate the use of trained police officers in both roles, arguing that it takes less time to train a competent helicopter pilot than an efficient police officer. However, there is general agreement that the observer should not be a pilot as he tends to watch how the pilot is flying instead of concentrating on watching the ground.

The bigger police helicopter units have their own maintenance organisations, but those with three or less machines tend to use an established local commercial maintenance facility.

There has been an interesting range of equipment used by police helicopters in their fight against crime. The simpler devices include gyroscopically controlled binoculars, video T.V. cameras, sirens, and public address loudspeakers. An interesting use of the latter occurred when a tanker went out of control due to brake failure and was spotted by the helicopter careering towards a series of traffic crossings controlled by signal lights. The helicopter came down low ahead of the tanker and warned all drivers to pull in to the road side and stop, thus averting a series of collisions.

Night flying is now a normal part of police helicoptering, and so their machines have been fitted with a 3.5 million candlepower 'night sun' light, which from the normal night patrol height of 700 ft (215 m) can light a 150 ft (45 m) radius, or the beam can readily be narrowed to a 20 ft (6 m) spotlight. This has proved a very effective device in combating night burglaries.

The London Metropolitan Police helicopters are equipped with a Heli-Tele air to ground television surveillance system, which has a remotely-controlled zoom lens operating from as wide an angle as 20° to as narrow an angle as 1°, thus enabling high magnification so that vehicles may be identified at distances of 1¼ miles (2 km) and individuals picked out of a crowd at distances of 650–1000 ft (200–300 m) for both discreet surveillance and positive identification. The action is displayed simultaneously in the aircraft and transmitted via a real-time video link to ground control.

British police have also used a compact, lightweight thermal imaging system based on a radically new sensor device that picks up infra-red wavelengths in the three to five micron range. The system consists entirely of the hand-held viewer/sensor unit and an accompanying shoulder-carried power pack. The device has located the body of a woman, who had died more than two weeks before.

Another device of a very different nature is helicopter rappelling. If police operations call for emplacement of a tactical team on a building roof, which is obstructed by chimneys or television antennae or is suspect for strength to receive the helicopter, then the police officers can lower themselves by rappelling down a 90 ft (27 m) rope from the hovering aircraft. This technique demands larger type helicopters than two-seaters.

One of the most efficient helicopter law enforcement units is that of the Baltimore City Police Department which is responsible for an area of 89 square miles (230 km²), of which the helicopter unit patrols the central 12 square miles (31 km²). Computer-based surveys showed that optimum cost-effectiveness could be achieved by operating from 09 30 to 01 30 and outside these hours on standby. Each crew is limited to five flight hours in an eight hour duty day, and a normal sortie lasts one-and-a-half flight hours. Reaction time from alarm alert to airborne is 90 seconds under normal circumstances; this is important as arrests go up as reaction time comes down. The helicopter unit answers 15 000 calls a year and assists in 100 arrests per month. This effort involves over 1000 flight hours per helicopter in a year.

Europe has been slower in using the helicopter for law enforcement purposes. France was first on the scene when the Gendarmerie acquired a helicopter from the Sud-Aviation company in 1954. In that year only 156 hours were flown, but by 1963 the number of helicopters had grown to 39, which flew 9776 hours. That utilisation is low, however, compared with the Los Angeles police helicopters, 7 of which flew 8000 hours in 1969.

The Yugoslav police are the latest European force to take delivery in 1979 and 1980 of 14 single-engine helicopters equipped with ambulance layout for use by local police in major metropolitan areas of the country.

This latest acquisition now means that virtually every European country has police helicopters, although some forces are of a para-military composition.

Even the railway police have taken to the air in helicopters in the U.S.A. The South-East Pennsylvania Transportation Authority has with the aid of a grant from the Federal Railroad Administration formed a Helicopter Police Patrol, which is mainly an anti-vandalism surveillance unit. The railway has been plagued with youthful stone-throwers, but with the introduction of the helicopter patrol there was a 30% decline in stone throwings in a year, a 38% reduction in the number of windows broken, and a 60% decline in the number of passenger injuries resulting from acts of vandalism. The helicopter has also prevented serious accidents by spotting obstructions laid on the rail tracks, and it has ejected many trespassers on rail property.

As far as records are available, it seems certain that no police department which has undertaken an evaluation of regular helicopter patrols has found them anything but successful in the fight against crime in giving invaluable assistance in the many tasks the police are called upon to perform in the course of their duties.

(B) Fire-fighting

The use of helicopters for fire-fighting has had wide application in open spaces such as forests, heathland and tundra, but has not found the same popularity in urban areas. To some extent this due to fire brigades regarding the helicopter as a rescue vehicle rather than fire-engine in the urban environment, and to some degree it is due to lack of helicopter specialist equipment for fighting fires in cities.

In spite of this, a number of major cities throughout the world have a helicopter fire unit – Los Angeles, Chicago, Paris, Tokyo and Hong Kong, although their helicopters are expected to play a dual role including rescue.

These cities use their helicopters to take fire crews up beyond the reach of fire ladders to the roofs of high buildings, to pull extra long hoses by the nozzle to awkward points which fireman have had difficulty in reaching, and to carry portable pumps to inaccessible places such as burning ships. In many cases their main role is that of reconnaissance and control, carrying a senior fire officer whose aerial perspective gives him the best vantage point for deploying his ground units.

In dealing with open space fires, reconnaissance and control again often plays a prime role, but the helicopter can really exploit its versatility in this environment.

The forest fire is perhaps the most dangerous of all fires, because of the

A Jet Ranger lifts a fire hose to a high tenement balcony

rapidity with which it spreads, the unpredictability of its path, and the difficulty in getting ground vehicles to the scene of operations. The first operational use of a helicopter to fight a forest fire was on 5 August 1947 in California, and it showed that it was the answer to the precept of speed of attack for effective fire suppression.

The first decade of helicopter use against fire was primarily logistic or support operations with the light piston-engine machines, although these recorded some remarkable feats, including the laying of 10 000 ft (3000 m) of fire hose from two Bell 47–G2s.

The entry of bigger helicopters into the field saw the scale of operations grow in the second decade, and at the 1959 Woodwardia Fire in Angeles National Forest, 3000 fire-fighters were moved; 56 000 U.S. gallons (212 000 litres) of water/borate dropped; and 45 tons (46 tonnes) of freight delivered. However, the biggest operation occured in the 1964 Los Padres National Forest fire in California, when 19 helicopters flew 1172 hours in 12 days, moving almost 9000 fire-fighters and 250 000 lb (113 400 kg) of freight, dropping 28 000 U.S. gallons (106 000 litres) of water and retardants, and laying 18 miles (29 km) of telephone line.

The third decade was marked by equipment development. Fixed external helitanks were increased in size and cascading efficiency, hover-fill buckets were likewise refined and enlarged, rappelling was introduced, and the cannon-spraying nozzle invented.

The most widely used device is the hover-fill bucket. At first these were of metal, then fibre glass, but now urethane rubber is used to allow compact stowage. A 2000 U.S. gallon (7570 litre) bucket with an electrically actuated bottom lift gate discharges its contents in 21 seconds.

Rappelling is used with the helicopter up to 250 ft (75 m) above the ground

A Jet Ranger demonstrates the water bomb method of fighting forest fires

Firefighters rappelling from a hovering Bell 205A of Evergreen Helicopters

and in winds up to 25 m.p.h. (40 km/h), and is tending to replace parachuting or smoke jumping as it is known to fire-fighters.

The idea of a self-contained package of motor pump, tank and cannon spraying nozzle was developed by Aerospatiale in France. Strangely enough it is a follow-on of a fire preventive device developed by Rocky Mountain Helicopters to wash the salt deposits off power line insulators in Utah to prevent the highly conductive salt crust causing current to leak into the pole tops setting them on fire quite often. An Aerospatiale Lama helicopter carried a 100 U.S. gallon (300 litres) water tank, a 300 lb/in^2 (21.1 kg/cm^2) pump, and a fixed nozzle extending 6 feet (2 m) beyond the rotor arc. In winds up to seven or eight knots a stream could be squirted accurately for a distance of 15 to 20 feet (5 to 6 m) on to the insulators with the helicopter hovering above and to one side of the target.

Another new development is that of night operations, as the night hours are generally the best conditions for fighting a fire, since temperature drops, humidity rises, and winds abate, but of course there is the matter of darkness. The use of night vision goggles, which intensify any light, both ambient and near infra-red, allow pilots to fly into extremely dark areas with sufficient accuracy to make water drops. However the goggles have only a 40° field of vision, and require considerable pilot acclimatisation.

A forward-looking infra-red device developed by the U.S. Army has proved very good in picking up hot-spots, which fire-fighters had believed fully extinguished, and are potentially dangerous in restarting the blaze. These hot-spots are shown to the helicopter crew on a cockpit television display.

The U.S. Forest Service is the biggest known user of fire-fighting helicopters, but it charters 97% of these from commercial operators. The other 3% are leased to allow the Forest Service pilots to remain proficient and check out contract pilots. The Service is expected to use 200 helicopters in 1980 and fly 30 000 hours. Its main areas of operations are California and Alaska. Contracts are arranged on a fixed hourly use rate with a minimum-availability guarantee.

The helicopter essentially supplements ground forces in fighting forest fires, and the general technique is to either contain the fire by encircling it, or to lay a barrier line to stop the fire's progress. The main value of the helicopter is its speed of reaction, and in some cases it has succeeded in laying the defence circle or line by itself particularly by use of chemical suppressants. The Russians used the wet line method very successfully in fighting tundra fires with the MIL 6 helicopter, which could carry 2600 U.S. gallons (12 000 litres) of fire retardants.

Another fire scourge area is the island of Sardinia where the shepherds are accustomed to deliberately burn the dried vegetation and brush so that the first autumn rains would cause the grass to grow more quickly. Often these fires get out of the shepherds' control and the fire helicopter patrol has proved an effective deterrent against this unlawful practice.

In certain specific cases such as an aircraft crash the helicopter can play a very vital role in controlling the conflagration to allow rescue of the crew and passengers. Firstly its reaction speed in arriving on the scene with fire-fighters and fire suppressants will determine survival chances, and then it can physically aid the operation by using its rotor downwash from a strategic position to blow flames and smoke away from the victims and rescuers.

There is little doubt that the acceptance of the helicopter in the fire-fighting role has been hampered by opposition from professional firemen, who either do not understand its potential or do not wish to understand, because they see it as a threat to their established meethods. This is not a new scenario in helicoptering, but just the slow phase in the re-education process.

(C) Air ambulance

The use of the helicopter as an air ambulance was pioneered militarily in the Korean War in the early 1950s. Experience of air evacuation of wounded from the battlefield to hospital in Word War II was very limited because only fixed-wing aircraft were available, but enough was undertaken to show that the effects of traumatic shock, which can cause critically wounded soldiers to die within minutes and seriously wounded ones within one or two hours depending on the type of wound, can be successfully countered if the victim can receive proper surgical treatment in time.

The death rate per hundred wounded in World War II was 4.5, but in the Korean War in which 15% were evacuated by helicopter this rate was reduced to 2.5, and in the Vietnam War some fifteen years later when massive use of helicopters allowed 90% to be air evacuated the rate was reduced still further to less than 1.0.

The Korean experience made its impact on the American civil population, who have been fighting a continuous battle of survival against the mayhem of automobile accidents. Since 1900 there have been well over one billion such accidents in the U.S.A. causing over two million deaths and some sixty million people to be injured. This is nearly three times the casualties suffered in all the wars in which the U.S.A. has been involved.

Although in Korea the helicopters used were often of such small types that the wounded were carried in Stokes litters affixed to the outside of the crew cabin, designers began to turn their minds to the rapid conversion of bigger helicopters to enable them to carry a number of stretchers and attendant medical personnel.

The first civil helicopter to be converted to an air ambulance was the Jet Ranger, fitted to carry two stretchers in addition to the crew and medical equipment. Its turbine engine gives it good speed of response. It remains the main type used as a civil air ambulance, although there are very few on full-time duty as such. The majority are police helicopters, which double as rescue vehicles, although they always give the latter task priority.

An air ambulance service is provided by the MAST (Military Assistance to Safety and Traffic) system to certain of the lesser populated states in the U.S.A. Some communities have also raised their own funds to sponsor an emergency medical helicopter service.

One of the most ambitious air ambulance schemes is Life Flight, which operates three Alouette 3 helicopters in the State of Texas over a radius of 130 miles (210 km) from the Texas Medical Center. The helicopters are operated by Aviation Medical Services, which is a subsidiary of a well-known American commercial operator. They are flown and serviced by eight pilots and four mechanics. The helicopters are on call twenty-four hours a day and can respond within five minutes. Each carries a doctor, nurse, and medical life-supporting equipment. In an emergency patients are transported regardless of ability to pay, but otherwise fees include a 10 U.S. dollar initial lift-off charge, 2 U.S. dollars per mile (round trip), 100 U.S. dollars per hour for all flights over two hours duration, and for medications administered during flight.

The use of such a service and indeed all air ambulance flights requires

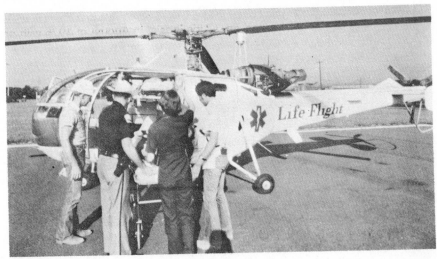

One of the Alouette 3s of Life Flight's air ambulance service

careful control to prevent unnecessary call-outs. Normally the police, fire brigade, ambulance service, and area doctors all have an authorisation call for this purpose.

Another necessary feature of an air ambulance service is a network of hospital helipads for direct access to general hospitals, casualty hospitals, burns units, and units specialising in dealing with brain damage, spinal injuries and premature babies. There are about 1000 such hospital helipads in the U.S.A. and Canada.

Certain classes of injury such as spine damage can lead to paralysis or death if the patient is jolted as is possible in a road ambulance. A large proportion of such injuries occurs in mountain climbing, and transportation over mountain roads is both rough, slow, and even precarious. In such circumstances the helicopter air ambulance provides the only humane alternative.

(D) Motorway patrol

Motorways are the modern equivalents of battlefields. The daily toll of casualties caused by aggressive drivers, timid drivers, careless drivers, incompetent drivers, and above all impatient drivers is truly appalling. The main killer is speed, sometimes too slow but usually too fast. There may be other factors involved, but excessive speed usually has the last say. Often that speed is criminally excessive.

These two factors, accidents and speeding, are both difficult to deal with in high density traffic conditions. The obvious solution is the motorway patrol helicopter, which is a combination of police, air ambulance, and emergency rescue helicopter.

A Jet Ranger air ambulance picks up motorway road accident victim

The Maryland State Police employ a system for speed detection from the air whereby one of the helicopter crew clocks the time an apparent violator enters a pre-marked quarter mile of motorway. The stop-watch is stopped as the vehicle exits. If the speed limit has been exceeded, a description of the offending vehicle is reported to a motorway patrol car, which makes the arrest.

The helicopter is also ideal for high speed vehicle pursuit if criminals are using a getaway car, as such pursuit eliminates the hazards to both police and public.

In the event of motorway accidents, often involving a considerable number of vehicles, it is difficult if not impossible to get police cars, ambulances, and fire vehicles to the crash scene. The helicopter can drop an officer to take incident control, give a situation report, and act as an air ambulance. It can also bring in rescue equipment and personnel, or specialist advisers as required, e.g. to deal with an overturned tanker carrying toxic chemicals.

Insurance companies have taken a great interest in such use of helicopters, and in Germany they helped to fund a Bolkow 105 helicopter for ADAC (the German Automobile Association) to patrol the autobahn near Munich. This was such a success particularly in the matter of life-saving that the system has been extended all over the country. On the spot treatment is given to accident victims by a medical team, and urgent cases are flown

ADAC Bo. 105 on autobahn patrol

direct to helipads on roofs of hospitals or in their grounds. The lives saved in this way amply repay the insurance companies for their investment.

In 1970 a study in Germany showed that every person killed cost insurance companies on average about £10000. Since the ADAC helicopters are considered to have saved 500 lives in their first three years of operation, then some £5 m can be credited to them. The capital outlay for the six Bo. 105s used was £780000 and the total cost of three years of operation was less than £2.5 m. Most of this cost is born by the Ministry of the Interior. ADAC now has ten Bo. 105s.

(E) Emergency rescue

In every country that operates military helicopters there is a Search and Rescue (SAR) unit. For example Great Britain's island shores are ringed with such units at approximately 100-mile (160-km) intervals round the coastline. These SAR units are always available to the civil population and indeed the great majority of their missions involve the rescue of civilians from the sea, cliffs, mountains, and indeed from some quite extraordinary locations such as the tops of factory chimneys and the bottoms of disused wells.

Although military or para-military units such as the U.S. Coastguards and French Protection Civile comprise the majority of emergency rescue helicopters, there are also a large number of purely civil units throughout the world – Swiss Air-Rescue mountain rescue helicopters, the British Airways

North Sea rescue unit, the Australian surf rescue unit, the Japanese Maritime Safety Agency helicopters, to name just a few.

The Swiss Air-Rescue is an independent, humanitarian, and charitable organisation with its headquarters in Zurich, and is the official auxiliary wing of the Swiss Red Cross. It operates eight Alouette IIIs and three Bo. 105s, all equipped with medical and rescue gear, and it utilises the fleets of private helicopter companies as well as relying upon its own fleet. With thirteen helicopter bases established, the Swiss Air-Rescue can reach the scene of any accident in Switzerland in fifteen to twenty minutes.

Swiss Air-Rescue is financed virtually by public subscription. For a charge of twenty Swiss francs a year, a subscriber is entitled to free emergency-medical transport. Family subscription is two-and-a-half times the basic charge. There is also a payback from insurance companies for many of the operations, where the subscriber has insurance that normally pays for ambulance services. In such cases the Swiss Air-Rescue bills the insurance company for a portion of the costs incurred.

Another unusual rescue/ambulance organisation, founded in 1946, is the Mission Aviation Fellowship, which is an interdenominational international agency providing aerial and communication support to overseas missions, especially in remote developing areas. Although it operates 120 aircraft in 22 countries it only started to operate helicopters in 1975, and now has five based in Mexico, Indonesia, Zaire, and Honduras, as well as a training machine at its headquarters in Ramona, California.

Individual rescues by helicopter are so varied as to almost defy description, but an outstanding example occurred in the early 1950s, when the then new Bell 47J four-seat piston-engine helicopter was being demonstrated in Lima, Peru. At that time news was received that the daughter of a Peruvian journalist lay critically injured in La Oroya, one of the highest villages in the world. Her injuries included fractured vertebrae and a broken pelvis, so she could not survive a mountain road journey. The Bell chief pilot, Joe Mashman, took off with auxiliary fuel, oxygen, and a stretcher and flew the 125 miles (200 km) to La Oroya, clearing the 17000 ft (5000 m) Andes en-route. He returned to Lima with the girl and a tumultuous welcome from 8000 people. For this splendid feat the pilot received the Peruvian Gold Medal.

Turbine-engine helicopters are able to cope with high altitude work much more easily, and in 1979 a Soloy Hiller plucked three climbers off Mount McKinley, Alaska, at a height of 18300 ft (5600 m). Heli-Orient operating the Helicopter Wing of the Royal Nepal Airlines Corporation, carried out 45 rescue missions in the lofty Himalayas in its first year of operations in 1972–3, using Jet Rangers.

Generally, civil helicopter emergency rescues are made by specially trained and equipped units under contract to undertake such duties, but there is a code of ethics among helicopter pilots that any emergency call receives priority over any other task. Such a call may come in the most unexpected way, such as in the case of the low hour private pilot flying his Bell 47G in the south-west of England, whose passenger spotted a man sunk up to his chest in quicksands. The pilot dropped the passenger on firm ground, then hovered over the struggling man so that the skid on the passenger side was within the victim's reach. The pilot then slowly pulled him clear and dragged him to safe ground.

Mass rescues are usually the result of natural disasters, when every available helicopter, military or civil, is mustered to give help. Floods such as that in Holland in 1953, and around Tampico, Mexico in 1955 when 9262 lives were saved by helicopters; earthquakes like that in Managua, Nicaragua, in 1972 when some 10 000 lives were lost and but for helicopters that number might have been double; snowstorms of the ferocity of that in the Chicago area of the U.S.A. in 1967 when helicopters provided virtually the only mode of transportation that could operate effectively; these are the occasions when helicopters literally become angels of mercy.

Helicopter rescue from the 1953 flood in Holland

Another type of disaster that is modern and man-made, and in which it is again a matter of all helicopters, military or civil, to the rescue is that of the terrifying high-rise building fire. If the fire occurs above the eighth storey it will be out of reach of fire brigade ladders, so any people trapped above that level will inevitably seek refuge on the roof.

Many such roofs are obstructed by air conditioning units, radio antennae, etc. and some are not stressed beyond about 32 lb/ft^2 (156 kg/m^2) which is only sufficient to take a five-seat helicopter in an emergency situation. Under such circumstances, helicopters may have to winch people to safety, or use ropes, or hover over the roof while people clamber aboard. All these methods are difficult operations which can be made positively dangerous if the people it is intended to rescue are in a state of panic. The first essential is therefore to lower someone to control those on the roof.

Even then the helicopter has the problems of heat and smoke to contend with. The ingestion of the heat from the flames may effect engine performance adversely, as well as causing turbulent updraughts, and the smoke may obscure visibility so that the pilot loses horizon reference or cannot see the roof. Experience has shown that it is better to fly under any smoke billowing over the roof rather than try to fly down through the smoke on to the roof.

There have been examples of such high-rise fire rescues all over the world. In April 1966 some sixty people were rescued from the Zim Building in Tel Aviv; in 1971 forty-three persons rescued in Mexico City; in November 1972 eight people lifted by two commercial helicopters from a seventeen-story burning building in New Orleans.

However, the three most massive fire rescues were in South America. In February 1972, the 31-storey Andraus Building in Sao Paulo, Brazil, was gutted by fire. Fortunately its roof had been designed as a heliport, and some 450 people were lifted off by eleven helicopters. The second such Sao Paulo fire rescue operation occurred two years later when 100 people were skilfully saved from the roof of the 25-storey Joelma Building, whose roof was so obstructed and weak that the helicopters could not touch down. As a result of these two episodes a new Sao Paulo city ordinance required that all new buildings more than 117 feet (35 metres) high have rooftop helipads capable of being used in emergencies.

Helicopter rescue from the roof of the burning Andraus Building, Sao Paulo

Survivors climb aboard the hovering rescue helicopter from the roof of the Joelma Building, Sao Paulo

A Bell 47J approaching the burning Avianca Building in Bogota.

In July 1973 some 500 people were rescued from the roof of the burning 40-storey Avianca Building in Bogota, Colombia by four helicopters. The fire started on the fourteenth floor and was detected from the air by a traffic patrol civil helicopter. This three-seat helicopter together with a four-seater from the same company started the rescue efforts and at the same time alerted the Colombian Air Force. Approximately half-an-hour later the Presidential Bell 212 and a similar Air Force helicopter joined the rescue operation. The roof of the building had originally been planned as a small heliport, but a 4 foot (1.2 m) high wall around the roof made things difficult. In addition Bogota is 8260 feet (2518 m) above sea level with a mean temperature of 60°F (16°C), so conditions were about as adverse as they could be, particularly for the small Bell 47 helicopters.

The three-hour Bogota operation was conducted superbly in these difficult circumstances, as the first helicopter to alight on the roof had uplifted two mechanics from its base who were briefed to control the panicky crowd awaiting rescue. The helicopters then dropped each load of rescued in the street, now cordoned off by police, and uplifted police, firemen, doctors, and equipment to the rooftop.

The lessons of these horrendous South American high-rise fires have not been lost on the Western world. Early in 1974 Los Angeles provided for rooftop landing zones for helicopters on buildings more than 75 ft (23 m) high. The city of Chicago followed suit by adopting a policy requiring buildings more than 80 ft (24 m) tall to have a rooftop clear zone by 15 April 1975. Both ordinances applied to new and structurally capable old buildings.

In the U.K. the City of London Police in conjunction with the British Helicopter Advisory Board set up a Helicopter Emergency High Rise Rescue Scheme in 1974, which involved a survey and plan of every high-rise rooftop in the square mile (2½ km²) business centre of London. In the event of a high-rise fire, a general alarm is broadcast from London Airport Air Traffic Control to every helicopter flying on the London Control Zone Helicopter Routes. The helicopters proceed to a prearranged landing area to pick up the roof plan as well as police and fire officers before proceeding to the rescue. The scheme has been exercised and refined from the lessons learned by rehearsals as well as from the experiences of Sao Paulo and Bogota.

Rescues at sea are often equally dramatic because they usually occur in stormy conditions that tax the courage and skill of the rescuers to the full. On 1 March 1976, the North Sea oil rig Deep Sea Driller struck an underwater rock while being towed into position in Norwegian waters. The rig keeled over 45° and the crew abandoned it in a liferaft in heavy seas. All 44 men were picked up by civil and military helicopters, which reacted very rapidly to the distress call.

The largest helicopter evacuation ever made at sea occurred on 15 December 1979, when unusually severe storm conditions in the North Sea snapped three of the twelve steel anchor cables holding the derrick barge 'Hermod' adjacent to a production oil rig. The captain of the barge decided to slip the remaining nine anchors as a safety precaution, but the action posed the possibility of a slow drift towards the Scottish coast. To avoid the problems of a full evacuation at night in worsening conditions, the captain called for an

The North Sea oil rig Deep Sea Driller after striking a rock in Norwegian waters

The crane barge HERMOD alongside the Texaco Tartan oil rig

emergency evacuation of the entire work force of 527 persons. Bristow Helicopters sent their Aberdeen fleet of 13 helicopters in winds gusting over 80 knots (150 km/h), frequent snow showers, and a 500 ft (150 m) cloud base. In the 40 ft (12 m) waves the 100 000 ton (101 600 tonne) barge was heaving 20 ft (6 m) vertically as well as pitching and rolling beyond normal helicopter operating conditions. To try and improve the stability of the barge the main cranes were cradled on either side of the helideck, requiring the helicopters to manoeuvre backwards to land. In spite of this, 25 round trips of two hours each were made over a seven-hour period to evacuate the 527 strong work force.

Rescue at night is still a difficult and often impossible task. It is particularly dangerous to attempt to hover in pitch darkness at about 100 ft (30 m) above the surface unless the helicopter is equipped with an automatic hover-hold device such as is fitted to naval anti-submarine helicopters with dunking sonar.

Helicopter landing deck on the crane barge HERMOD

A somewhat different facet of emergency rescue is that of rushing blood plasma, snake-bite serum, or transplant organs from 'banks' or donors to hospitals. The helicopter is ideal for this door to door purpose over short ranges, especially as the cargo itself is very small.

The Swiss helicopter company Air Glaciers has set up its own rescue insurance system for an annual premium of 20 Swiss francs per person, or 50 Swiss francs per family. This insurance covers rescue, and rapid evacuation in the event of skiing or mountaineering accidents or car accidents on mountain roads, and even includes rapid transfer to a hospital in an emergency. It also covers searches for missing people or animals. These premium rates guarantee operating activity up to a cost of 10 000 Swiss francs.

There is no doubt that in the field of saving human life, the helicopter stands supreme as a versatile rescue vehicle. The incredible contribution it has made is illustrated by the fact that the first recorded mercy mission was on 3 October 1944, when a U.S. Coast Guard Sikorsky R–4 helicopter flew a cargo of blood plasma to a U.S. destroyer which had suffered an explosion injuring more than 100 of the crew. In 1977 the U.S. Coast Guard helicopters flew 74 637 SAR missions.

It is not possible to count the number of lives that have been saved by the helicopter but it has been estimated that for every helicopter built, at least seven lives have been saved.

A large number of rescues are called for as a result of incompetence or foolhardiness of yachtsmen, swimmers, mountain climbers and potholers, but occasionally a completely bizarre rescue can occur, which involves none of the usual elements. Such an event as initiated by the escape in September 1980 of the tame T.V. advertising star grizzly bear, Hercules, while on location in the Outer Hebrides islands of Scotland.

The 785 lb (352 kg) animal obviously enjoyed its new found freedom, but there were fears for its ability to survive. After vanishing for some 22 days it was spotted very much alive, but slimmed down to a mere 350 lb (240 kg). A civil helicopter happened to be visiting the islands and gave chase after picking up the bear's owner and a veterinary surgeon with a tranquilliser dart gun. The wily Hercules proved an elusive target, covering three miles at some 20 m.p.h. and using great tactical evasive skill till finally put to sleep, when he was netted and returned in somewhat undignified style as an underslung load to his travelling cage, where he recovered none the worse for wear.

Hercules being netted for underslung load

Chapter 9

Scheduled services

If this chapter was entirely devoted to the success record of the helicopter in providing scheduled services, it would probably be the shortest in the book, because the history is one of trial and error, and mostly the latter. There are logical reasons for the failures, and sound grounds for future optimism.

The first helicopter scheduled passenger service was inaugurated in 1950 by British European Airways Helicopters* between Liverpool, Wrexham and Cardiff using 4-passenger Sikorsky S–51s. This was superseded in 1951 by a service between Birmingham, and Northolt and Heathrow airports in London. Then in 1952 a service between London Airport and Southampton was operated with three 4-passenger Bristol Sycamores. All of these services were withdrawn after a few months, because they were not economically viable. The reasons for this non-viability were essentially the lack of big enough passenger-carrying capacity aircraft, and the lack of regularity due in the main to weather.

Meanwhile in the U.S.A. in mid-1953, New York Airways started a service with three 7-passenger Sikorsky S–55 helicopters between John. F. Kennedy International, La Guardia, and Newark airports, and Wall Street Heliport. This service had a federal subsidy to support it.

In 1954 BEA Helicopters, still undeterred, ran a service from central London to London Heathrow airport with three S–55s. However, British regulations dictated that the helicopter must follow the Thames through central London, and because the S–55 was single-engined it must carry flotation gear, which so adversely affected payload that the service was soon withdrawn. It was switched to the industrial Midlands to operate between Leicester, Nottingham and Birmingham, but was withdrawn at the time of the Suez crisis due to the fuel shortage.

BEA helicopters made two major decisions based on these experiences. Firstly, only to use twin-engine helicopters on scheduled services, and secondly to develop an all-weather capability for such operations. In the event it was not till 1961 that BEA Helicopters (BEAH) was able to conduct trials with a twin-engine helicopter, when the military Bristol 192 tandem rotor aircraft was loaned to it.

By late 1954 Los Angeles Airways was running a scheduled service from the main airport to the sprawling surrounds of that vast city. In late 1956 Chicago Helicopter Airways set up a scheduled service between the city

* British European Airways formed a Helicopter Experimental Unit in 1947, which formally became BEA Helicopters on 1 January 1964.

centre and the two main airports of O'Hare and Midway. Both these services were federally subsidised in order to demonstrate the feasibility of urban operation of rotorcraft. In about 1960 a non-subsidised service started up in Boston.

In Belgium the national airline Sabena operated a helicopter scheduled service between 1954 and 1967. It was a feeder line to and from Brussels linking it with Liege and Maastricht in Belgium, Cologne and Bonn in south-west Germany, Amsterdam and Rotterdam in Holland, and Lille in north France. In addition to the three passenger routes there were two postal routes. All services stopped at Brussels city centre and called at Brussels Airport.

The service started with S–55s and eventually was equipped with eight S–58s. In the first five years of operation 53 000 hours were flown. However, the service suffered from insufficient passenger capacity in the helicopters and the lack of full all-weather capability to make it economically viable.

The Chicago and Boston operations also petered out, the former after the virtual closure of Midway Airport, but two new scheduled services arose in the mid-1960s when the 26-passenger Sikorsky S–61 appeared on the market. The payload of this helicopter offered a marginal chance of economic viability, so in 1964 BEAH took the plunge, followed a year later by San Francisco–Oakland Helicopter (SFO) Airlines. The latter was mainly an inter-airport service between San Francisco International and Oakland International.

Success story

In May 1964, BEAH purchased two S–61s and allocated one to take over the main BEA airline operation from the Cornish mainland to the Scilly Isles. BEA operated three De Havilland Rapides from the small airfield of St Just to the equally small airfield of St Mary's in the Scillies, and carried less than 28 000 passengers per year.

The Scilly Isles lie 28 miles (45 km) south-west of Land's End, the south-west tip of England, and consist of five inhabited islands and over a hundred uninhabited smaller islands and rocks. The climate is unusually warm for England, and so there is a flourishing tourist business in spring, summer, and autumn. The islands have an extensive flower industry, and because of the mild winter climate there flowers bloom two weeks ahead of those on the mainland. There is therefore the basis for a viable helicopter passenger service for three-quarters of the year, and a good cargo element in spring and winter, when in an average season 800 tons (813 tonnes) of flowers amounting to 50 million blooms are exported. Nevertheless the situation appeared finely balanced when BEAH decided to put only one S–61N on the service with no back-up, although it purchased two of the helicopters.

This courageous or, as it seemed to many, foolhardy decision was made on purely financial grounds, as the service could not bear the standing charges of a second S–61. However, 10% of the second helicopter was allocated to cover the periods of major overhauls.

BEAH's all-weather experience was now brought to bear on the route, and the company noted that the regularity of the Rapides was considerably affected by sea fog which plagued the 250 ft (75 m) high St Just aerodrome. It therefore decided to set up a heliport near Penzance rail terminal. The town is right on the coast and is connected by a first-class rail service to London. Its harbour also has a steamship connection to the Scillies.

The ten-acre (four-hectare) heliport is virtually at sea level and this has allowed a 98% regularity, which is well above that achieved by the Rapides. The truly superb aspect, however, has been the availability of the S–61N running in excess of 99%. For periods of up to six months a 100% engineering regularity has been continuously maintained during the peak summer operations.

The British Airways Helicopters S-61N on the Penzance–Scilly Isles scheduled service embarks passengers at Penzance Heliport

The service operates six days a week, with Sundays devoted to maintenance, and in the summer there are twelve flights a day out of Penzance and twelve from the little airfield on the island of St Mary's. This reduces to one or two return services daily in winter. The round trip takes 40 minutes, and is flown at 1000 ft (300 m) at a speed of 120 knots (222 km/h). There is a five minute turn around involving disembarkation and embarkation of 34 passengers and baggage, and refuel at Penzance with rotors running. Check-in for passengers is only a twenty minute routine.

The service operates to special VFR limitations because of the geographical location of the operation. The limitations are a cloud base of 300 ft (90 m)

above the landing pad and 985 yards (900 metres) RVR (Runway Visual Range). The principal navigation aid is Decca, backed up by ADF and VOR/ILS. Weather radar and a radar altimeter are also fitted.

In the first year of operation 47765 passengers were carried on 2346 journeys. The number of passengers soon increased to about 58000 per year, and stabilised there for some years. The limiting factors were the S–61N passenger capacity of 28, and number of hotels, and the length of the season in the Scillies. However, the passenger capacity of the helicopter eventually rose to 34 as a result of an allowed increase in aircraft maximum weight and revised seating arrangements, and also the agreement of the island hoteliers to lengthen the season was obtained.

In 1973 when BEAH became British Airways Helicopters a total of 64560 passengers were carried on 2970 journeys. By 1975 the total had passed the 70000 mark, and in 1978 a total of 80000 were carried on 3784 journeys. In June 1979 the millionth passenger was carried.

This scheduled service operation has been described in some detail because it is successful in making a profit. The successful ingredients are to offer a service to which there is no attractive alternative; operate an aircraft with a high passenger capacity; estabish a high regularity rate of operation; ensure there is an all the year round demand and not a seasonal one only.

In the case of the Penzance–Scillies service the alternative method of transport is in a small steamship, which has a shallow draught to suit Penzance harbour, and therefore rolls heavily in the Atlantic swell on the three-hour trip to St Mary's; the 34-passenger S–61N with a 98% regularity has proved ideal for the task; and the passenger demand covers three of the four seasons, and cargo sees the operation through the lean winter.

Feeder services

The feeder type scheduled service in metropolitan areas to or from a major airport or between two or more airports serving the same centre is a different ball game, and this is where most of the 'casualties' have occurred in the matter of collapse of the operating companies. The maximum number of passengers ever attracted to such a helicopter service has been 1¼% of the total moving through the airport terminals.

When New York Airways (NYA) was operating the 26-passenger Boeing Vertol 107 to and from the roof of the Pan Am Building it carried 327000 passengers in 27 months. This is an economically viable operation for 1½ helicopters with an annual utilisation per machine of 1800 hours and an average load factor of 40%. This is computed by multiplying the helicopter passenger capacity by 4000 to give the required number of passengers to be carried per year.

When that operation ceased in February 1968 because of a contractual disagreement between the operator and the rooftop heliport owner, NYA changed over to the Sikorsky S–61L of which it eventually purchased four.

These made 62 daily departures from the three airports they served, at intervals of 30 minutes. Over 35 000 passengers were carried in the first eight weeks of service, and soon there was a regular uplift of 6000 passengers weekly. It reopened operations on the Pam Am roof on 1 February 1977, but an unfortunate ground accident on the roof terminated the operation three-and-a-half months later. It continued to operate to Wall Street Heliport, but an in-flight accident in 1979 brought NYA operations to a complete halt, albeit temporarily.

After its government subsidy expired in 1965, NYA showed its only profit in 1972. It estimated that it could show a profit with a 46% load factor and was heading that way in 1978 with a 45.4% load factor, and doing even better in 1979 when the fatal accident occurred. In 1978 NYA flew 4 930 000 revenue passenger miles, a 7.5% increase over 1977. Seat miles flown totalled 10 077 000.

There are certain factors in this type of scheduled service operation which are necessary for success. Firstly the frequency of helicopter operation must be greater than two flights per hour throughout the travelling day. Secondly, the break-even load factor should be no greater than 40%. Thirdly the utilisation should be between 1400 and 2200 flying hours per year. Fourthly two helicopters of the same type will be required on line during peak travel hours (07 00–09 00 and 15 00–18 00), and only one during the remaining time.

The NYA's suspension of operations have given it breathing space to review these precepts, and their intention was to acquire four 17-passenger Aerospatiale SA330J Pumas. This smaller passenger capacity should be almost fully taken up, if their previous experience is anything to go on. However, the ghosts of Los Angeles Airways, which went out of business in 1976, and San Francisco–Oakland Helicopter Airlines which were liquidated in 1977, must be haunting the NYA planners.

By a quirk of fate British Airways Helicopters acquired the SFO's three S–61s, and has itself gone into the airport feeder type scheduled service, but not in the full contractual sense. The British Airports Authority (BAA) which runs London's two main airports of Heathrow and Gatwick purchased a Sikorsky S–61N in 1978, which it leased to British Caledonian Airways, one of the main airline operators in the U.K., who in turn arranged for British Airways Helicopters to operate it. The service is subsidised by the BAA and carried 58 000 revenue-giving passengers in its first year.

This is purely a link service between the two airports, which are 25 miles (40 km) apart, but have congested road connections, although a motorway is being constructed. The service operates ten return flights daily and is planning a fully IFR operation with Microwave Aircraft Digital Guidance Equipment (MADGE). The break-even factor is a 60% payload. The 15-minute flight is flown partly at 2400 ft (730 m) and partly at 1300 ft (395 m), the latter sector being in the busy London Control Zone.

In late 1978 the U.K. saw its third scheduled service born, and this a rather unusual one in the modern scenario. A Jet Ranger is operated by Burnthills Aviation between Glasgow Airport and Fort William, a small but key town in the Highlands of Scotland. This service is subsidised by the Highlands and Islands Development Board, and is a VFR operation with only five return flights per week. In mid-1980 it is being extended to two return flights per weekday, one of which will continue to be direct, but the other will have intermediate stops at the Clyde resort of Rothesay, the beauty spot at Loch Gilphead, and the west coast resort of Oban.

The American experience with scheduled helicopter services is confined to inter-airport operations in the main, and these have proved to be so delicately balanced with regard to profitability that withdrawal of the supporting subsidy or the befalling of a misfortune tipped the balance. In the Chicago case the concentration of commercial airline operations at O'Hare; in the Los Angeles case two helicopter accidents; in the San Francisco case a paralysing strike by mechanics; in the New York case two helicopter accidents. All these were recipes for commercial disaster.

The European experience has been more diversified but it is too early to say whether it is truly more successful. The Belgian operation lived on a subsidy and died on the wrong equipment; the Scillies operation keeps its head above water and BEAH maintains a remarkable safety record throughout this and its extensive North Sea operations; the Gatwick–Heathrow Airlink has yet to prove it can live without its subsidy; the Glasgow–Fort William exercise has set up a new game whose rules have yet to be written to see if they make economic sense, for it is a unique venture in every sense of these words.

In the Far East there have been temporary scheduled services in Pakistan and Japan, but these were discontinued after brief runs.

The monopoly situation

Greenland, the world's largest island, and a most hostile piece of terrain hardly seems a likely place to find a scheduled helicopter service, and yet Greenlandair runs one of the largest of such operations. Its eight 22-passenger S–61Ns serve sixteen towns and villages along the mountainous west coast with a total route length in excess of 1740 miles (2800 km). Like the Belgian operation it is primarily a domestic feeder service to Sondre Strom Air Base, with its headquarters at Godthaab, the island capital. It is a day VFR only operation, with the longest single route stage of 195 miles (314 km) barely possible in the few twilight hours of winter. The mountainous terrain and low flight profiles render VHF communications ineffective, so HF has to be used. Yet in spite of these drawbacks the Greenlandair operation has succeeded, because it meets the necessary prerequisites for success, and above all there is no alternative mode of travel. Since 1965 the service has flown 90 000 hours, and in 1978 lifted 40 000 passengers – almost equal to the population of the entire island.

Future prospects

From this chequered pattern of world-wide scheduled service operations the question of whether there is any optimism for the future must be asked. There are really two scenarios to consider – the urban inter-airport service, and the overwater or longer range service. From experience to date the former seems the more difficult to get right, so let us start by examining its potential for success.

If the service is purely inter-airport and does not include a city centre stop, the most important factor in customer demand is frequency and regularity of service. The fare cost does not play as vital a part as one might imagine because it represents a comparatively small percentage of an airline passenger's total fare outlay. Such a service may therefore be best equipped with a number of medium size turbine helicopters.

If a city centre connection is included in the inter-airport service, then the site of the urban heliport plays its part as a success factor. The more truly central it is in the sense of being adjacent to main rail and omnibus terminals, the business and shopping centres, and metropolitan hotel complexes, then the more it will attract customers and such a service will probably require larger helicopters. Since noise generally increases with helicopter size this in turn makes it more difficult to acquire an environmentally acceptable urban heliport site.

The overwater/longer range type service has basically a greater potential for success as a scheduled service. First and foremost it must offer a much more attractive mode of transport than the alternatives if indeed there are any.

Short-haul passengers are more demanding of higher frequency service, since it is not worth-while for example to wait several hours for a one hour trip, but in spite of this dictum the statistics show that an aeroplane journeys up to 250 miles (400 km), 51%–65% of the total trip time is spent on the ground. However 250 miles (400 km) is about the limiting range at which helicopters are competitive with aeroplanes in terms of journey block time, and only because they eliminate the city centre to airport journeys at each end and also they offer shorter check-in and check-out times. If the stage length is reduced to 100 miles (160 km) or less the percentage time spent on the ground still remains the same for the aeroplane, and so the helicopter becomes increasingly more attractive since its block journey time is now very much shorter.

If we look at the two successful helicopter scheduled services now operating in Greenland and England we see that they offer route stages mainly below 100 miles (160 km) and the alternative mode of transport is unattractive. In each case too the frequency of service is geared to demand, and suitably-sited urban heliports are available.

British European Airways Helicopters has also learned from its experience on the Scillies route that, as with aeroplanes, provided the demand justifies

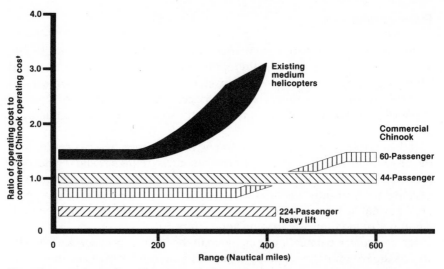

Operating cost comparison of passenger helicopter types

the operation of larger aircraft then the economics of the service improve as
the aircraft size grows. In consequence BEAH has been waiting for the right
size helicopter to launch its projected scheduled services network between
London and the continental capitals of Paris, Brussels and Amsterdam. The
advent of the European Economic Community (EEC) has made this project
particularly attractive from a passenger demand standpoint as there is now a
commuter market for the routes.

The Sikorsky S–65 helicopter would have been capable of carrying 46
passengers for 285 miles (460 km) at a cruising speed of 172 m.p.h. (277 km/
h), but this civil version of the military CH–53 was never built. Now the main
contender is the 44-passenger civil Chinook, already ordered by BEAH for
North Sea operations, but likely to be stretched to a 60-passenger version for
scheduled services.

The 44-passenger Commercial Chinook operated on a scheduled service
over a 200 mile (320 km) route segment would have a break-even load factor
of about 55%. If the 60-passenger version was used it would offer a 25%
reduction in seat mile costs. It is also possible to build a wide body version of
the helicopter to carry 224 passengers, and it could compete favourably with
fixed-wing aircraft on short range operations. Its seat mile cost would be
only one-third that of the 44-passenger version.

With such a large capacity helicopter the EEC scheduled service begins to
look very promising, but in the first instance the 60-passenger version would
seem viable provided centrally sited heliports can be found in the capitals.
Obviously they are unlikely to be in the heart of the cities, but as long as they
are considerably nearer the centre than the international airports and can
offer all-weather facilities the game is on.

In London a start has been made to find the right site for just such an operation, and an area of London's disused dockland is being safeguarded for the purpose. The site is on the east side of the capital and will have good road and underground rail connections to the centre with about a 15-minute travel time. Similar sites are likely to be available in Paris and Brussels, although Amsterdam may be more problematical.

Actually a demonstration flight in a CH–53 was made in April 1970 from Battersea Heliport on the west side of London to Issy-les-Moulineux Heliport in Paris. Time for the journey was one hour twenty minutes with a block time of two hours from city centre, as against a block time of three-and-a-half hours by the conventional air service. The helicopter's block time should be improved on by some twenty minutes if starting from a London Docks heliport.

On aeroplane journeys between 250 and 500 miles (400 and 800 km), 39%–54% of the total trip time is spent on the ground. Modern technology helicopters are moving into the 400-mile (640-km) range, but the speed performance will have to be stepped up into the 200 m.p.h. plus (320 km/h) order to make them competitive on scheduled services of that distance.

Potential testing ground

Perhaps it would be interesting to conclude this chapter by looking at a potentially favourable area for helicopter scheduled services and examine why it has potential and if so why it has not been exploited to date.

Scotland is a country of tremendous scenic beauty with its famed highlands, lochs and offshore islands, as well as being a golfer's paradise and indeed the birthplace of the game, while it is also opening up winter sports facilities, so it is a tourist attraction of the highest order in spring, summer and autumn. However, it is a land of severe winter weather with short hours of daylight, and its islands lie in the turbulent waters of the mighty Atlantic ocean. Add to these pluses and minuses the fact that the surface communications over the northern and western part of the country are both sparse and inadequate. The railways have been severely reduced for economic reasons; the roads are narrow and hilly and often impassable in winter; the islands are served by small steamers whose regularity is often severely restricted by Atlantic storms.

Scotland has an air network, which runs at a considerable financial loss mainly due to under-utilisation of the outlying airfields away from the major cities. If it is accepted that fixed-wing airports are required at the major cities of Glasgow, Edinburgh and Aberdeen, then closure of the others in favour of a helicopter network covering ten islands and eight towns in the north and west of the country is a distinct possibility.

The economic aspects of such a scheme make sense since the running costs of eighteen heliports would be very much less than those of comparable airfields designed to accommodate fixed-wing aircraft. The structure of the scheme is flexible enough to ring the changes as the seasons and the demand dictate. However, to date the essential equipment has been missing – a large all-weather helicopter. With the advent of the Commercial Chinook the potential is now realisable.

Although in some ways such a scheduled service bears resemblance to that in Greenland, the difference lies in the tourist and North Sea oil related traffic potential in Scotland. Also while some sectors of the network could sustain a large helicopter all the year round, others would only merit a medium helicopter particularly in the winter. There might therefore be a requirement to subsidise part of the operation.

The interesting thing is that the starting gun has been fired by the initiation of the Glasgow–Fort William scheduled service. This is a modest probe to what could become either a very large operation or just another damp firework in the history of helicopter scheduled services.

Another venture which will try and rise phoenix-like from the ashes of the New York Airways near success is that of New York Helicopter Corporation, a subsidiary of New York's Island Helicopter Corporation, which in late 1980 restarted the scheduled services between Kennedy, La Guardia and Newark airports to Island's heliport in midtown Manhattan.

Initially the airline is using four 9-passenger Dauphin 2 helicopters, although it is aiming to incorporate in its plans the lessons learned from New York Airways and acquire 20-passenger Super Pumas. The helicopter world will watch with interest to see if this formula will prove correct or just another pipe dream.

Chapter 10

The air taxi and the dual trainer

The chartering of helicopters as air taxis is perhaps the most mundane of all helicopter operations, but it is still the backbone of the small operator sector of the industry. It is not without its glamour, for the helicopter is a mode of transport favoured by actors and actresses, politicians, T.V. personalities, racing drivers, jockeys, and many other sports starts. It offers a time-saving way to leap over the heads of the crowds that attend their functions, and it also offers a unique form of security.

The range of charter uses is almost unlimited – for weddings, transport to grouse shooting moors, lifting skiers to mountain tops, taking cruise passengers out to the ship they have missed, bringing Santa Claus to a Christmas party – the list is endless.

One operator in Scotland takes foreign visitors on tours of that country's famous golf courses, so that in one day they can play a round at the historic St Andrews, the breathtakingly beautiful Gleneagles, and the championship Turnberry, thus spanning the width of the country from North Sea coast to Atlantic coast.

Charter rates are usually by the flight hour, and to this must be added positioning time and landing fees. Waiting time is not normally charged, but there will be a minimum flight time of one hour per half day or two hours per full day. If the actual trip is less than one hour it will be charged on a pro rata basis.

An extension of the air taxi service is pleasure flying, joy-riding or sightseeing trips – call them what you will. These are usually associated with some special short duration event such as an air display, town fair, business convention or seaside promotion. However, not all such operations are one night stands, and two very successful year round operations are to be found in the U.S.A.

Location is all important and must adjoin a permanent attraction. In the case of the Island Helicopter Corporation that attraction is the New York skyline. By offering a unique view of a unique city, this company carries over 35 000 sightseers per year, most of whom are making their first helicopter flight. The people themselves are of course as important as the attraction. There must be plenty of them in a non-recurring sequence, since sightseers tend to do it once only.

Commodore Helicopters of San Francisco carry 75 000 sightseeing passengers per year from Fisherman's Wharf round the fascinating bay area for four-minute trips. Unlike the New York operation, which presells about

A sightseeing Jet Ranger over Sydney Harbour

The air taxi helicopter at an English conference centre

half of its flights as part of a foreign-tour package and relies heavily on foreigners to make up 80%–85% of its business, the San Francisco operation has no prebooking, but just a steady stream of interested clients.

Experience has shown that the equipment used should have passenger seating in multiples of two, as couples make up the majority of passengers and will not be separated into different helicopters. Back-up aircraft are also essential since the large number of take-offs and landings involved make a heavy demand on the maintenance side of the operation.

There are a considerable number of seasonal 'flightseeing' operations going on around the world, but many of them have been jeopardised by

A charter helicopter about to take-off from Westland London Heliport

being one helicopter operations and the wrong type of helicopter at that.

In normal air taxi operations the pilot often finds himself in unusual, out of the way situations, where he has to use his initiative in arranging to get fuel supplies and weather information. This latter problem has been solved in England, renowned for its unstable weather, by the introduction of a General Aviation Visual Flight Forecast Service. This system divides the country into thirty areas and provides telephonic information on essential meteorological data. A pilot requiring a route forecast calls the number for the area required and gets the information by Automatic Telephone Answering Service. The data is given in an order which conforms with a pro forma supplied free to pilots, flying clubs and commercial operators.

The air taxi business is prevented from flourishing on the European mainland by the restrictive regulations whereby off-airport landings require written exemption from the national body controlling civil aviation in some countries. At one time in France any such landing required the permission of the landing site owner, the gendarmerie, and the prefecture. This state of affairs has now improved in France, but none of the continental countries exhibit the realistic freedom of operation that exists in the U.K.

One aspect of air taxi business which is unwelcome is the hijack risk. Because of the short range of helicopters this is a low risk, but the helicopter does offer certain attractions to terrorist groups. It has been used for prison break-outs, aerial bombing, and robbery getaways. However, criminals

Bo. 105 air taxi landing on rooftop helipad of the International Press Centre, London

seem wary of the helicopter, probably because they do not understand it, and also because helicopter pilots have more opportunity for initiative in thwarting the hijackers, because of the flight characteristics of the helicopter.

The all-weather helicopter should be a decided asset to air taxi operators, as it will expand their capability to ensure fulfilment of any charter commitment, and this reliability factor will weigh heavily in the operators' favour.

Flight instruction

In the main helicopter user countries of the world, the commercial sector is supplied with pilots from the military sector, where they get a thorough and sophisticated training at the taxpayers' expense. In consequence civil flying training schools have largely had to depend on foreign students and a few private students to survive commercially, and therefore such schools are limited in number.

Private pilot training

Because of the high capital cost of the helicopter there are relatively few private helicopter owners and thus few private helicopter pilots in the world.

However, the advent of a cheap helicopter could change this situation.

Almost all light helicopters in existence are capable of being fitted for dual instruction, and ab initio training is usually undertaken on the two seat piston-engine types. These are generally more difficult to handle than turbine-engine types, because there is no automatic throttle/pitch control, i.e. the engine and rotor r.p.m. have got to be synchronised. Also these small helicopters have not got such a good power/weight ratio as turbine helicopters, so students get a sound grounding in the dangers of overpitching, probably the most common and dangerous mishandling fault that a pilot can perpetrate. Because of this piston training, pilots find conversion to turbine helicopters relatively easy, as the latter have automatic throttle control and a good power/weight ratio.

The most difficult thing for an ab initio pilot to learn is the art of hovering, and since this is a new dimension for fixed-wing pilots the latter are often slower to master it than students who have never flown aeroplanes. In general, however, the time from first helicopter flight to solo varies between eight to twelve hours, which is similar to that for aeroplanes.

The total helicopter flight time required to gain a Private Pilot's Licence (Helicopters) is normally 40 hours, of which 20 hours must be dual instruction. There is a concurrent ground school syllabus covering such subjects as Air Law, Flight Rules and Procedures, Navigation and Meteorology, Rotorcraft Aerodynamics, and knowledge of the airframe and engine of the specific type for which the licence will be valid.

A PPL(H) does not entitle the holder to fly for hire or reward, and normally restricts the holder to undertake visual contact flying only.

Commercial pilot training

There are two grades of professional pilot licences: the Commercial Pilot's Licence (Helicopters) and the Airline Transport Pilot's Licence (Helicopters), the difference being mainly that of relative experience. However, there is a move afoot in the International Civil Aviation Organisation to have only a single Professional Pilot's Licence, with specialist ratings, e.g. agricultural, flying instructor, etc. superimposed on that licence after undergoing training and tests to gain the necessary rating qualifications.

Training for a CPL(H) is again usually done on two-seat piston-engine aircraft. I use the word aircraft deliberately, for out of the 150 flight hours usually required, a proportion may be done on a fixed-wing aeroplane, but normally that proportion is limited to 50 hours. The ground syllabus covers the same subjects as for the PPL(H), but additionally includes Flight Planning, Navigation Plotting, Radio Aids, Signals and Radiotelephony.

On completion of the CPL(H) the student is still a low-time pilot and generally will have to build up experience on light helicopters or as a co-pilot on twin helicopters before his services are widely marketable, and indeed an Instrument Rating will probably be an essential in this respect.

Autorotation practice

Virtually all helicopters are sold with dual control as an optional extra for conversion training and continuation training, and one of the key exercises that all helicopter pilots have to practise regularly is that of autorotation landing. The skill involved in this manoeuvre comes in determining the correct altitude to begin the flare, and the rate of flare to arrive at the preselected ground point and preselected height as close to zero speed as possible with sufficient rotor r.p.m. available to cushion the final vertical descent. Timing is therefore the essence of a successful autoration, and obviously there is room for human error.

In consequence the helicopter pilot world is evenly split into two schools of thought on whether or not autorotation landing practice should be taken the whole way to touch-down or terminated at the flare to zero speed by opening up the throttle and taking-off from that point. The pro touch-down school argue that there is no substitute for the real thing, while the anti touch-down group maintain that the cure is worse than the ailment and that more helicopters are damaged in practice than in real emergency landings, for besides the pilot judgement required in the matter of timing, most helicopters are very sensitive to non-level attitudes and sideways draft at touch-down.

Suffice it to say that the U.S. Army, who were strong protagonists of the full touch-down, made a study of all emergency autorotations over a two-and-a-half year period and found that 50% were unsuccessful, so the obvious conclusion is that the full touch-down practice is no guarantee to success when the real thing happens. Significantly enough the study does not reveal the ratio of successful to non-successful full touch-down practices.

Quite apart from the accident risk, the weakness in the pro autorotation practice argument is that such practices are usually conducted from straight and level, unaccelerated flight at approximately 60 knots (111 km/h) and 500 feet (150 m) above a flat, hard surface, and for a very restricted range of aircraft gross weights, centre of gravity positions, and density altitudes. This set of conditions is rarely met in the real thing.

Flight simulators

The answer to the problem is probably to devise an autorotation simulator, in which one could explore autorotation performance boundaries without fear of an accident. Although simulators are commonplace in the civil fixed-wing world, they are just coming into their own in the civil helicopter field. The information transfer from simulator to actual flight has proved to be of such quality that the civil aviation authorities allow a considerable percentage of simulator hours to replace flight hours for pilot certification and qualification.

The commercial helicopter industry's prime need in the simulator field is for a low-cost model such as Analog Training Computers' ATC–112H, which in 1978 was selling for less than 15 000 U.S. dollars. The original simulator was not enclosed, but this option became available on later models. It is based on a turbine-engined helicopter, and the pilot can adjust the pneumatic cyclic control sensitivity to match the type he wishes to simulate. It has an IFR instrument panel and a very limited autorotation mode. The machine is not designed to teach hovering and doesn't register speeds below 40 knots (74 km/h). It also has a wheels up/down mode for those who fly helicopters so fitted, and the main rotor blades can be set for clockwise or counterclockwise rotation effects.

The capabilities of this type of simulator are limited to navigation and basic IFR procedures, and specific flight areas of 50 by 75 miles (80 by 120 km) can be fed into the simulator computer by printed circuit programmes. Additionally a very realistic ATC tape can be run, giving continuous transmissions between the controller and other aircraft, so the student not only has to fly the simulator, but also be alert for his call sign.

The operating cost of this procedural trainer once it is started up was only 3 U.S. cents an hour on 1978 prices, that is about the same cost as to light a 40 watt domestic bulb.

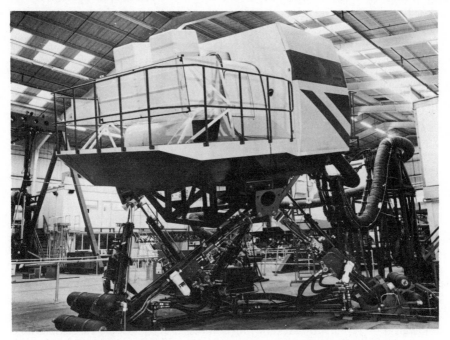

S–61 six axis simulator

At the other end of the cost scale is the sophisticated six axis S–61N helicopter simulator built by Redifon Flight Simulation in the U.K. The first model was built in two years for British Airways Helicopters at a cost of £1.8 m including the building in which it is housed, and put into service in early 1979. An actual S–61N cockpit was used to reproduce the real machine's true responses to sounds and vibrations, and the whole mounted on a six degree of freedom support motion system which can recreate all the sensations experienced in an actual helicopter, such as pitch, roll, surge and sway. It also has a computer generated visual system, which gives a night/dusk image through two front windows. The resultant view of any selected airfield is incredibly realistic with runway, aerodrome, and adjacent town lighting. An oil rig image at sea, is also available. Because of visual limitations, hover and landing are not easily executed. There is a choice of 150 system faults that can be applied, many of which cannot be demonstrated in the actual aircraft.

The capital cost of such a simulator approximates to that of the actual helicopter, but the operating cost is of course much smaller and errors by trainees do not involve expensive repairs. The safety factor is an obvious advantage, but the operational and commercial advantages are the important gains.

The possession of such a simulator would mean that aircraft which would normally be required for training are freed for commercial operations. In BAH's case their 160 pilots had to average four hours each year on training checks in S–61s, thus taking the aircraft out of commercial service for 640 hours. In addition the S–61s were used for a further 400 hours training the 40 recruit intake each year. In effect therefore some 1000 hours were lost each year, which with ad hoc charter rates for the aircraft at £1000 an hour in 1979 amounted to about £1 m in potential revenue being lost. On this basis more than half the total cost of the simulator could be recouped in the first year.

In actual fact the simulator has a potential utilisation of 3000 hours per year, operating a five-day week for twelve hours per day with a 98% serviceability. The operator can therefore not only meet his own training requirements, but sell time to other S–61 operators.

The simulator also offers availability advantages independent of weather, time of year, or operational schedules. It also eases environmental problems by taking aircraft out of the local airfield circuit especially at night, and reduces general airspace overcrowding.

There can be no doubt of the value of both procedural and full IFR simulators, which can meet the approval of the civil aviation authorities for flight time in them to count as time in the air towards licence qualifications. For a large number of exercises, simulators can offer more thorough training than in the air, because the instructor has more exercise parameter control and can both repeat any exercise and demonstrate some which are impossible to demonstrate in the air.

In 1980 BAH ordered the first tandem rotor helicopter simulator in anticipation of the delivery of the first of its Chinooks in 1981. Redifon Flight Simulation will build the new model.

Chapter 11

Rotorcraft safety

The most important aspect of any aviation undertaking is safety of operation. Without it there can be no commercial success, no military efficiency, no public acceptance. It involves everyone – designer, manufacturer, operator, pilot, maintenance engineer, meteorologist, air traffic controller, refueller, and even the hangar floor sweeper.

In this safety scenario the helicopter has its pluses and its minuses, but examination will show it has more of the former than the latter.

Accident rates

If we look at where the helicopter stands today in statistical terms as a safe form of transport we will see that on a size and weight basis it has more accidents per 100000 hours of flight time than its fixed-wing counterpart, but less fatalities. This latter fact points to the potential of the helicopter to be the safest of all aircraft.

The helicopter accident rate over the five years 1973–7 has averaged 18 per 100000 hours in the U.S.A. and slightly less in the U.K. The fatal accident rates were 2.3 and 1.26 respectively. Significantly there has been a steady decline in both these rates in both countries over the last ten years.

The aviation risk in comparison with other risks both in every day life and for self-imposed hazards are:

	Death risk per hour of exposure per million
Bus U.K.	0.03
Rail U.K.	0.05
Private car U.K.	0.6
Passenger flying	1.0
Motor cycle U.K.	9.0
Canoeing	10.0
Mountaineering	27.0
Motor cycle racing	35.0
Rock climbing	40.0

If twin-engine helicopter accident statistics are looked at in isolation, the figures in the U.K. show a startling improvement on the overall figures. The accident rate over five years has averaged 3.86 and the fatal accident rate 0.3. This is a remarkable record when it is considered that the helicopters involved did virtually all their flying over the hostile North Sea to offshore platforms.

There are four sectors of operation in which helicopter accidents mainly occur:

(a) *Non-commercial private flying:* Most operators of these aircraft do not fly or practise often enough to maintain the proficiency needed to handle emergency situations.

(b) *Agricultural application:* Crop spraying is an inherently dangerous operation.

(c) *Power line and pipeline patrol:* Low speeds and altitudes, and high obstacles leave little margin for corrective action in the event of an emergency.

(d) *Dual instruction:* Although it has only half the accident rate of private flying, it is obviously a high risk sector cushioned only by the experience of the instructors.

The types of accidents to helicopters show a clear statistical pattern:

	Per cent
Engine failure or malfunction	30
Collision with wires or poles	11
Hard landing	10
Roll over	10
Controlled collision with the surface	8.5
Uncontrolled collision with the surface	8.5
Collision with buildings, etc.	7
Nose over	6
Collision with trees or crops	5
Tail rotor failure	4.5

The causes of helicopter accidents show an equally clear pattern:

	Per cent
Pilot error	76
Terrain	36
Powerplant	20
Weather	13.5
Mechanical other than engine	13.5
Maintenance or ground personnel	11

Note: More than one cause may be attributed to an accident, so the percentage exceeds 100.

From this latter table it will be seen that the human factor plays a major role in any accident, so it is interesting to get a breakdown of how significant pilot experience is when related to accident percentages:

	Per cent
51–100 hours	13
101–500 hours	34.5
501–1000 hours	11.5
More than 1000 hours	19

The pattern in this table is less complex than at first sight. The beginner pilot after a cautious start moves into an area of over-confidence, frightens himself and eventually matures till he passes into the major group of pilots where he gets all the tough assignments.

The average risk of travelling by air on a journey as compared with alternative methods of transport will depend on the total time of travel. When account is taken of the average speed of helicopter travel as compared with road, the journey risk by road is about four times greater than by helicopter.

Safety in design

Armed with this statistical data let us examine the safety question in more depth. The helicopter is a young innovation in aeronautical terms, so has not had so much time to develop itself as the aeroplane, but as happened to the aeroplane the helicopter is now going through an accelerated period of technological development. The designer therefore is having a peak opportunity to influence safety, and some of the more obvious results are seen in such devices as the fenestron tail rotor and fibreglass main rotor blades. However, the matter of safety in design is much more than skin deep.

The manufacturer is of course responsible for both design and production, and has a specialist design team consisting of specialist cells to deal with design areas such as rotor blades, transmission systems, fuselage structure, landing gear, engine layout, etc. and all co-ordinated under a chief designer or project leader.

Analysis of malfunction reports by operators shows that 21% of such reports deal with the main rotor system, which includes blades, hubs, gear boxes and transmissions. This pinpoints one of the fundamental weaknesses of the helicopter in that a main rotor gear box or transmission failure is worse in effect than an engine failure, because even on a twin-engine helicopter there is only one gear box, and it is an additional hazard on helicopters which is not present on aeroplanes. However, having said that, the incidence of such complete failures is very low in new technology helicopters.

The most catastrophic occurrence is of course a main rotor blade failure and this again is extremely rare. A few modern helicopters have fail-safe systems on the rotor retention system, but most have single spar blades depending on fail-safe characteristics such as skin cracks which normally occur as advance warning and are slow to propagate into the primary load-carrying spar, so are discovered on ground inspection. Some have pressurised spar inspection methods such as the Sikorsky S–61 BIM (Blade Inspection Method) system. During manufacture the blade spar is pressurised and sealed with nitrogen. Loss of pressure, which could be caused by incipient failure of the spar is clearly indicated by a colour gauge on each blade. With this system main rotor blades do not have a fatigue life but are retired on condition. There is also a cockpit BIM warning for the pilot.

Rotor blades

The big break-through in blade technology has been the use of fibreglass composite material replacing the wooden and metal blades of earlier designs. The first such blades were certificated by Messerschmitt-Boelkow-Blohm (MBB) in 1970 on the Bo. 105 helicopter. The fibreglass blade became a practicable solution when polyester resin as a bonding agent was replaced by epoxy-resin bonding, and has bestowed on the helicopter a marked performance increase and better specific fuel consumption at high weights. Above all, however, the fibreglass blade has infinite life and has thus increased the safety factor to virtually perfect reliability. For an equal weight of material the epoxy–fibreglass combination is much stronger than steel, light alloys or even titanium. The fibreglass composite blade also produces a lower vibration level, which in turn extends the effective life of other components – another safety bonus.

The hingeless rotor was inspired by the fibreglass composite and MBB produced the semi-rigid rotor on the Bo. 105, which gives incredible manoeuvrability as well as increased stability.

Gear boxes

The main advances in gear box design have been the reduction of components, and since the Achilles heel of the helicopter is its large number of moving parts, this change must improve safety. For example the Alouette 2's transmission contains 22 gears and 23 bearings, while the AS–350 Squirrel has only nine gears and nine bearings.

The duplication of oil pumps as in the Sikorsky S–76 should solve the basic problem of losing gear box oil, but in any event this helicopter's transmission should operate for four hours in the event of loss of transmission oil because all bearings are rolling elements instead of bushings.

Chip detector warning devices on gear boxes are now becoming standard fittings to supplement transmission oil pressure warning lights.

Engines

Engine failures have declined with the introduction of turbine engines with fewer moving parts, and much of this is due to effective warning of imminent trouble by oil sump chip detector warning systems.

The stamp of reliability is particularly high on the French Turbomeca engines, and their new Arriel turboshaft design has an engine assembly of five modules, which are independent units capable of being fitted to any engine. Modular separation is simple and allows easy access to the axial compressor, centrifugal compressor, gas producer turbines, power turbine, reduction gear box, and accessory box. This modular design allows maximum utilisation of the Time Between Overhaul (TBO) of each component. Current TBO levels are in excess of 2000 hours.

There is no doubt that twin-engine helicopters have demonstrated an accident rate lower than single-engine helicopters by a factor of about two. However, the probability of an engine failure is significantly higher for a twin but the consequences are of course normally much less serious.

Tail rotors

Tail rotor failure presents the pilot with his most difficult emergency situation from a handling standpoint. The vital role of the tail rotor in providing anti-torque to that generated on the fuselage by the main rotor as well as providing directional control for manoeuvring makes it a critical safety item. Mechanical failure of the tail rotor leaves the pilot with a situation where the helicopter will spin in the opposite direction of rotation of the main rotor (U.S. designed helicopters have counterclockwise main rotors, while European designs have clockwise main rotors). The only way to save such a situation of tail rotor failure in flight is to have enough height to autorotate and pick up speed so that the tail boom and fin will act as a directional stabiliser, but this speed cannot be reduced so there must be enough ground space for a run-on landing.

In spite of helicopter designs such as the co-axial and tandem rotor concepts, which eliminate the tail rotor, the vast majority of designs still have the conventional tail rotor, so safety is being improved in this area by the use of composite blades and by improving tail rotor gear box design.

The tail rotor has also proved a lethal weapon to unwary ground crews, careless passengers, and inquisitive spectators, who fail to see the fast rotating disc and walk into it usually with fatal results.

There have been two methods attempted to alleviate this menace. The Aerospatiale company has developed the fenestron or shrouded tail rotor, which has less yaw impulse than the conventional type and therefore requires a considerable fin area, but this in turn gives directional stability at lower speed in the event of a tail rotor failure. The other method is to raise the tail rotor to give increased ground clearance, but this usually involves introducing an intermediate tail rotor gear box at the angle of the boom carrying the tail rotor.

Performance improvements

The designer is not only incorporating the more obvious technological improvements, but improving performance features that affect safety, such as reduction of the avoid area of the height–velocity curve, giving the helicopter a substantial (say 20°) slope capability, a $-\frac{1}{2}g$ capability by use of hingeless or articulated rotors, and good hot and high out of ground effect hover capability.

Crashworthiness

Crashworthiness is also an essential aspect of designing for safety, and an example of this is the Hughes 500, which has an outstanding accident record in its class, much of it due to the egg shape of its fuselage which has shown itself to give the occupants a high survivability factor.

Although the pilots wear full safety harness in civil helicopters, the passengers, as in airline practice, wear lap straps only. However, in the smaller helicopters one or two passengers may be seated up front with the pilot, and they are expected (or in some instances compelled by law) to wear full harness.

Human responsibilities

In the production of helicopters, the manufacturer can best make a contribution to safety by good quality control at all stages of construction. He also has a responsibility to oversee any sub-contractors in this respect, and to make sure that only bona fide distributors sell approved spare parts.

The helicopter operator bears the real brunt of responsibility in the matter of accident frequency, because he employs the maintenance personnel and the pilots. Although possibly not involved in the initial training of both groups, he is responsible for their continuation training and organisation. It is a generally accepted fact in the industry that a helicopter operator is only as good as his maintenance organisation, for if he has put that side of his house in order it is certain he will do likewise with the flying side. Of course if you want top notch personnel you have to pay top prices and that brings us to the undeniable fact that quality is never bought cheaply. This fact is emphasised by the statistical turnover rate of 15% per year for licensed helicopter engineers and pilots in offshore operations.

This turnover rate reflects the adverse field conditions that are often associated with helicopter operations. In order to achieve a high utilisation of the aircraft, much of the maintenance has to be done on evening and night shifts, thus giving an unsocial life pattern.

With the tremendous increase in offshore oil and gas related support operations and agricultural operations, corrosion has become one of the helicopter maintenance engineer's nightmares. Helicopters require minimum overdesign factors for weight reasons, so high strength, low weight structural materials appeared at first sight to be a boon to the industry, but many of the alloys produced were very corrosion prone. It was also found that highly stressed metals can influence the severity of the corrosion process.

The direct chemical reaction type of corrosion, such as happens with battery acid and exhaust fumes, is much less common in helicopters than electrolytic corrosion. The latter involves two dissimilar materials and an electrolyte such as water, whose conductivity gives a reaction similar to that in a battery. The anode (positive terminal) gets progressively consumed while the product of the electrolysis becomes deposited on the cathode (negative terminal). Some metals are more prone to become the anode than others, with magnesium heading the list.

The manufacturer tries to combat possible pitting, intergranular or fretting corrosion by plating, sealing, priming and painting, but all of this is aimed at standard operating conditions. In offshore, agricultural, and tropical operations it is up to the operator to establish a proper corrosion control programme. Thorough and constant visual inspection, frequent washing with approved solutions, backed up by non-destructive techniques such as ultrasonic scanning and the use of dye penetrants will all help to prevent corrosion getting a grip. Such a programme may require as much as 25% of all maintenance man-hours being spent on corrosion-related activities.

All available statistics show that the pilot is blameworthy in about 76% of all accidents. That does not imply that he is always totally to blame, but he may have a share of the blame in a large number of cases. For example if an engine fails on a single-engine helicopter the pilot has to resort to an emergency autorotation landing, and if well executed the aircraft should be intact, but if he gets it wrong then varying degrees of damage can result.

There is always going to be a certain element of human error in aviation, but much of the potential error element can be removed or reduced. In the past the feeling has been that the whole answer lies in training, but it is now appreciated that there are many other factors involved.

On the medical and psychological side a considerable amount of research has been made on pilot fatigue and stress problems. It is now known that instrument flying, limited visibility conditions, monotony of operation, cockpit comfort, and vibration all affect pilot efficiency, and as a result there are now legal flight time limitations imposed on pilots of public transport helicopters. The science of ergonomics or cockpit environment has a very recent history, but is now recognised as playing an important part in accident prevention.

Whilst in the area of the cockpit, the operators are now coming round to the view that certain items such as the collective and cyclic control levers could be standardised in an effort to eliminate the kind of accident that emanates from familiarity of a push-button that is the force trim button on one type being the external load jettison button on another type with which the pilot is less familiar but has occasionally to cross operate within his company. The accident potential in this situation is obvious.

Researchers of human behaviour tell us that we are all subject to biorhythms, whereby our biological clocks regulate physical, intellectual, and emotional performance in a series of cyclic patterns, of 23, 33 and 28 days respectively, with positive and negative phases. When passing from one phase to the other we have our critical days when the statistical chances of having an accident are higher than on non-critical days. This theory is at a very early stage of research, but already significant results have been identified to support if not prove the validity of it.

If control of this sort could be exercised on pilots and maintenance engineers it might be a breakthrough in improving safety standards, but the practicability and commercial implications of such a system seem formidable.

Two piloting problems that have come into prominence in the 1970s are icing and vortex wake turbulence. Icing has come to the fore because of the advent of helicopter IFR operations.

From a safety angle the main danger with ice build-up is the resultant performance loss. The change in aerofoil shape on the main rotor blades caused by ice accumulation gives a loss of lift and an increase in drag, and the resultant loss in overall rotor thrust has to be compensated for by increased collective pitch, which in turn compounds the drag problem and so calls for disproportionate increases in torque and power requirements. At the same time increase in fuselage drag requires yet another power increase to maintain airspeed. This situation may eventually force the pilot to reduce height to maintain control on a twin-engine helicopter.

Although single-engine helicopters have more restrictive IFR operating conditions imposed on them, their problem in the event of icing trouble may force them into autorotation, and the effect of rotor blade icing is likely to be a serious degradation in autorotation performance. The steady state rate of descent can be doubled in relatively light icing conditions.

Another unpleasant effect that can be caused by icing is asymmetric shedding of ice from the blades. This can result in mass imbalances that produce unacceptable levels of vibration.

These are the things that can happen but seldom do, because civil helicopters have strict certification limits for flying in icing conditions and these are dictated by the anti-ice protection equipment fitted. Since blade protection systems are very costly both in money and weight, they are generally not fitted to civil helicopters, but anti-icing systems for engine inlets and windshields are standard on most public transport helicopters.

The problem of vortex wake turbulence is a two-headed one for helicopters as it is for aeroplanes. Every aircraft produces an amount of disturbed air in its trail and other aircraft flying through that turbulent area before it has dissipated will be subjected to turbulence, the severity of which will vary with the size of the generating aircraft and the size and proximity of the affected aircraft. The pilot of any helicopter therefore has a safety duty to avoid flying in another aircraft's wake danger area, and also to avoid creating a problem by overflying another helicopter manoeuvring near the ground.

The non-skilled workers associated with helicopter operations must be encouraged and indeed trained to have an awareness of safety measures that can be taken by them not only to protect themselves in the execution of their duties, but to protect the safety of the helicopter in its flight tasks. For example the refueller must make sure that the right type and quantity of fuel is put in the aircraft. Obvious? – maybe, but Murphy's law may be in operation and the wrong type fuel has been put in the base installation by the fuel road delivery driver. Similarly in field operations, where fuel from portable drums or containers may be used, the refueller must scrupulously check for fuel contamination by water.

At the beginning of this chapter mention was made of the hangar floor sweeper, and indeed he has a task which demands conscientious application to ensure that nothing is left lying about in the hangar and apron areas, which could cause Foreign Object Damage (FOD) by being sucked into engine intakes or blown into rotor blades by the rotor wash circulation.

The part played by air traffic control in the matter of flight safety of helicopters is in effect the same as for fixed-wing aircraft, but the slower speeds and heights flown by helicopters pose a problem in their integration with fixed-wing traffic. However, this is a traffic flow handling matter, which has only cropped up in the 1970s with the coming of IFR helicopters and the solutions are gradually being evolved.

It might seem to the reader that helicopter operations are fraught with safety pitfalls, but it should be clearly understood that the elimination of the hazards is very much a winning battle and not a losing one. This is emphasised by the excellent records, particularly in the field of public transport of the British and American commercial helicopter operations, which are flown by crews who have almost all been given the superb training of a military pilot or engineer. This situation is also true of many other nations following a similar pattern.

To sum up, there is good reason to believe that technological advances will increase the reliability and safety of the helicopter to a degree, which in the case of the large twin-engine helicopter should by the early 1980s give an accident rate equivalent to airline safety standards of one major accident per 100 000 flight hours.

Chapter 12

Environmental problems

Noise has plagued the development of the helicopter insofar as it has slowed its acceptance to operate from urban heliports. Environmentalists, often well intentioned but given to exaggerated claims to further their cause, have exploited the emotional atmosphere that surrounds the issue of noise, till it has now become clouded with controversy and ignorance.

It is important that the problem of helicopter noise should be understood by the designer and operator as well as the layman, because the helicopter's future is intimately linked to how close it can operate to people.

Noise measurement

Sound is a rapid variation in atmospheric pressure, and travels in waves emanating from the source. These waves impinge on the eardrum which vibrates in sympathy and we hear sound. The human ear is constructed to sense both the magnitude (level) and the frequency of pressure waves. The response to these pressure fluctuations is not linear but logarithmic, so that if the magnitude of the pressure fluctuation is doubled the noise we hear is by no means twice as loud.

One of the great difficulties with noise is quantifying it, and although many different methods exist for measuring noise none of these is perfect. However, they are all an improvement on qualitative assessment, which is notoriously unreliable and can vary enormously from person to person, and can even be affected by psychological aspects. In this latter respect the helicopter is a particular sufferer for most people regard it as something which is available only to people who move in a different social strata, so they resent its presence – unless it is coming to rescue them.

The unit used to describe the level of sound pressure is the decibel (dB), and to correspond to the sensitivity of the ear it is non-linear. It appears in various guises for application to different noise sources. Community noise levels are usually quoted in terms of the 'A' weighted sound pressure level (dBA), which weights the noise level measured by a microphone so that it corresponds very closely to the sound heard by an observer. As examples the following values are typical of London:

Parks and gardens: 50–65 dBA   Main roads: 70–88 dBA
Residential roads: 65–85 dBA   Arterial roads: 72–92 dBA

If the same unit of measurement is applied to road transportation we get the following maximum values:

Motor cycles: 90 dBA   Motor cars: 87 dBA   Heavy vehicles: 92 dBA

If applied to helicopters the comparison is as follows:

Jet Ranger flying overhead at 500 ft (150 m) at 80 m.p.h. (129 km/h): 65 dBA

Jet Ranger in the hover at 33 ft (10 m) altitude, and measured 330 ft (100 m) to the side: 83 dBA.

The American Occupational Safety and Health Agency tables the following permissible human exposure limits:

90 dBA	8 hours	97 dBA	3 hours
105 dBA	1½ hours	110 dBA	¼ hour

The dBA has not been the ideal measurement unit for aircraft noise as it does not adequately measure the human reaction to noise annoyance. Perceived noise level expressed as PNdB takes into account the distribution of the frequencies that make up sound and correlates well with subjective judgements of the noisiness or annoyance of various types of sound. A very rough rule of thumb to convert dBA is to add 13 to get the value in PNdB for flyover conditions, and add 9 for hover. Some comparative values of road, rail, and air transportation in perceived noise decibels are:

Motor car at 50ft: 72–85 PNdB
Motor cycle at 50 ft: 90–102 PNdB
Diesel freight train at 50 ft: 109–112 PNdB
Jet Ranger at 250 ft: 80–86 PNdB
Bell 47G at 250 ft: 92–106 PNdB
4-engine Jet Transport at 700 ft: 118–123 PNdB
(1 ft ≡ 0.3 m)

From these comparisons we can learn some interesting generalities, namely that a Jet Ranger's noise would be unobstrusive on the ambient or background noise of the average big town or city, that turbine-powered helicopters are quieter than piston-powered helicopters of comparable size; and that the helicopter is pound for pound the quietest form of powered aircraft, partly because the helicopter noise is more localised.

There are other general statements that can be added from experience. It is well known that a high frequency sound seems louder and is generally more disturbing than one at a lower frequency, even though the decibel level of each may be the same. The duration of sound is also a factor than can disturb some people, and the helicopter has an advantage in this respect over surface transport. An unfamiliar sound will also attract attention, and its novelty may have a disturbing effect on many people. Another feature of noise that commonly causes annoyance is variability, so that a sound that is modulated in intensity or frequency is sometimes more annoying than is a similar steady sound.

The unique sound of a helicopter is readily identifiable, even when its perceived level is below the ambient level. This is due in part to the modulation produced by the relatively slow-turning main rotor, and in part to the fact that it emanates from the air rather than the ground level of most common sounds.

In assessing the acceptability of helicopters for city centre operations it is important that the noise tests be conducted at the site proposed to be used, for there are many factors such as high walls that may blank or bounce noise, and of course the ambient noise should cover the time of day at which it is intended to operate.

Helicopter noise criteria and certification

The Greater London Council has laid down noise criteria for helicopters using London heliports, requiring them to be capable of operating within a noise level of 81 dBA when measured at right angles to the flight path and at a horizontal distance of 500 ft (150 m) from the take-off or landing point. This limitation is also tied in with a limit on the number of movements (take-offs or landings) per year, excluding emergency flights, and also on the maximum allowable number of daily movements.

Westland London Heliport which is noise-monitored by the GLC

These noise criteria when compared with the 90 dBA talked of in the 1960s show a stiffening of requirements by some 9 dBA, which in effect means a halving of the acceptable noise standards of ten years ago.

This trend shows the challenge the industry is facing, and indeed the first steps have been taken in ICAO towards noise certification of helicopters. This has introduced yet another noise measuring unit, the EPNdB (Effective Perceived Noise Level), which more adequately accounts for blade slap, a subjectively disturbing noise of an impulsive nature caused by the near passage of vortex shed by one blade to a succeeding blade. It is only a severe problem on two-bladed main rotor helicopters and tandem helicopters with large blade overlap. However, the EPNdB cannot be readily converted to other units of noise.

The standards for noise certification of helicopters of new design after 1 January 1980 are as follows:

Reference condition	Up to 800 kg	800–80 000 kg	Beyond 80 000 kg
Approach	87 EPNdB	3 dB increase	107 EPNdB
Take-off	86 EPNdB	for	106 EPNdB
Flyover	85 EPNdB	doubled weight	105 EPNdB

(1 kg ≡ 2.2 lb)

The flyover consists of level 500 ft (150 m) overflights at approximately cruise speed. The landing must be flown along a constant 6° glide slope. The take-off is standard in procedure. Each flight mode must be flown over a three-microphone array at a specified airspeed, rotor speed, and maximum design gross weight. A noise level value is then calculated by averaging the readings of the three microphones and six runs.

It is not required that all three conditions be met. If the helicopter type fails on one then it is required to add all three together and if the total error is not in excess of 4 EPNdB then it is acceptable, provided any single condition excess is limited to 3 EPNdB. For example:

	Certification limit	*Type A*	*Type B*
Take-off	86	89	88
Flyover	85	85	85
Land	87	86	90
	258	260 – acceptable	263 – unacceptable

With the introduction of helicopter noise certification the gauntlet has now been well and truly thrown down in front of the designers, who are in a good position to take up the challenge thanks to modern technology.

Helicopter noise sources

The main noise sources in helicopters are:

(a) *Tail rotor:* This is the main source of noise in a modern helicopter. The noise is generated by the high velocity of the blade tips, which approach the speed of sound. It has been demonstrated that tail rotor noise can be significantly reduced by decreasing the tip speed and increasing the number of blades of the tail rotor. There is of course a weight penalty for such modification and this in turn might give a centre of gravity problem in a small helicopter.

(b) *Main rotor:* The problem is similar to that of the tail rotor and can be alleviated in similar fashion by decreasing the tip speed and increasing the number of blades. It is estimated that a 3 dB reduction in noise from the rotor by such modification would result in a 10% loss in payload. However, a redesign of the blades can give significant reduction in noise without a performance penalty. Boeing-Vertol estimate that the Commercial Chinook with its fibreglass blades will show a reduction of 13 EPNdB in comparison to the standard metal-bladed military model in a 500 ft (150 m) flyover. This improvement is mainly due to the transonic thintip aerofoils with increased blade twist. However, the economic penalties associated with basic redesign can be very high.

(c) *Blade slap:* This can be reduced in steady flight by adopting particular flying techniques, but although all helicopters can generate blade slap in some regions of flight, it does not occur to any major degree on helicopters with three or more rotor blades on a single mast.

(d) *Engine:* Exhaust mufflers are the obvious application to current engines, but they tend to introduce severe weight penalties. They are particularly effective on piston-engines, and such an installation on a Bell 47G claims a 43% noise reduction. Other modifications tried include shrouded engine inlets to suppress main-rotor transmission noise, and finer tooth gears. However, the engine designers have made big steps forward with noise suppression on jet engines of large transport aeroplanes without significant performance losses, and this is probably the easiest of the helicopter noise problem areas to tackle.

Noise abatement

To give an idea of what can be achieved on a present-day model and the penalties involved, the Hughes 500 was modified with regard to the tail rotor, main rotor and engine, and achieved a 78% decrease in noise for a 32% loss in payload, which would require a 23% increase in horsepower to compensate.

The helicopter pilot can do much to minimise noise by intelligent flight planning when in urban areas, and particularly in the approach and landing phase by use of a noise abatement technique to reduce blade slap. The technique requires the pilot to establish a rate of descent of at least 500 ft/ min (150 m/min) *before* reducing airspeed, then airspeed is reduced to about 70 m.p.h. (113 km/h) while increasing rate of descent to at least 800 ft/min (240 m/min), or alternatively the rate of descent is held to less than 200 ft/min (60 m/min) while reducing airspeed to about 65 m.p.h. (105 km/h), then the rate of descent is increased to at least 800 ft/min (240 m/min). The 800 ft/min (240 m/min) rate of descent should be held at between 60 and 90 m.p.h. (97 and 145 km/h) unless the main rotor tends to slap, when the rate of descent may be increased. On approaching the flare, the airspeed should be reduced below 70 m.p.h. (113 km/h) before decreasing the rate of descent. Normal flare and landing should then be executed.

The noise of helicopters, unlike that of road traffic, can affect all the surfaces of a building, and so some concern has been expressed that buildings might be damaged by energy transmitted acoustically. Experiments have in fact shown the possibility of such damage to be negligible. For example a block of flats was fitted with resonance detectors to measure the vibration induced by a helicopter flying over at an altitude of 1000 ft (300 m). The detectors fitted on windows gave no response.

In the London Control Zone, which covers an area of 320 square miles (830 km^2), helicopters are required to follow designated routes, which are selected after consultation with the operators and local authorities. These routes are chosen primarily with a view to safety in the event of an emergency landing, and also to avoid noise-sensitive areas. Fortunately the two objectives are compatible and the routes have functioned satisfactorily with only minor changes over the last ten years. A similar system was introduced in the Glasgow Special Rules Zone in 1976.

The most built-up area of central London and the City, covering an area of 80 square miles (207 km^2), is prohibited to single-engine helicopters unless they fly within the high water marks of the River Thames on transit. This means that any central London heliport has to have either a landing and take-off platform out in the Thames or be a floating unit in the river.

There is no doubt that the helicopter industry is making every effort to improve its environmental image, because city-centre heliports are essential to the growth of helicopter transport in particular. The public must be educated in the problem and not raise emotional opposition based on no sound evidence. Studies have shown that there is a correlation between air travel and business development nationally, so it is important that everone appreciates what the real issues are in the matter of city heliports.

Exhaust pollution

An unfounded fear that people have about helicopters is that of associated exhaust pollution. Turbine engines, which power virtually all helicopters with more than three seats, produce less pollution per pound of fuel burnt than spark ignition engines used in road vehicles, because the air-to-fuel ratio on a turbine engine is much higher relatively than the reciprocating or piston engine. Also there are no lead additives in aviation turbine fuel, unlike petrol which gives a lead discharge when burned.

A Jet Ranger operating from a helipad emits 1.37 lb/h (0.62 kg/h) of carbon monoxide, 0.13 lb/h (0.06 kg/h) hydrocarbon as a hexane, and 0.35 lb/h (0.16 kg/h) nitrogen oxide. The equivalent values for vehicular traffic are 673.5 (305.5), 57.92 (26.27) and 21.52 (9.76). It is worth noting that the exhaust from a turbine engine is relatively low and the effluent is very quickly diluted and dissipated by the rotor downwash.

The environment of the helicopter crew and passengers is also a matter of much technological study. Internal noise of course affects the efficiency of the crew and the comfort of the passengers, and much can be done by sound proofing the cockpit and cabin using standard noise deadening materials.

Vibration

However, the real internal environmental problem besetting the helicopter is that of vibration. Although it is difficult to compare vibration levels of different transport modes because subjective criteria for complex vibration have not been agreed, the following typical triaxial R.M.S. accelerations in vehicles at cruising speeds give a reasonable comparison. The vibrations are given in metres/s^2 (1 m/s^2 $\equiv$ 3.28 ft/s^2).

Vehicle	Fore and aft	Lateral	Vertical
Military helicopter at 100 knots (185 km/h)	0.75	0.95	1.35
British Rail electric train	0.36	0.68	0.27
Car at 50 m.p.h. (80 km/h) on motorway	0.46	0.50	0.96
Single decker bus at 10 m.p.h. (16 km/h) in city	0.37	0.42	0.81

It can clearly be seen that the helicopter shows up worst of all three axes, with the vertical vibration most noticeable. Now the normal criteria in designing helicopters is to examine the vibration at various discrete frequencies and ensure that they are below set levels.

The helicopter vibrations from main and tail rotor result from aerodynamic excitation, and harmonics of 2/rev., 4/rev. and 6/rev. are normal and there are no main rotor adjustments for these. Higher frequencies are especially dependent on loading.

Variations in vibration can be caused by various factors such as r.p.m., airspeed, gross weight, centre of gravity location, ballast location, temperature, power, and condition of isolation systems such as pylon mounts and dampers, but these factors do not change the harmonics.

Vibrations of the two per rev. type can be affected by temperature change. 15°F (8°C) change can make a noticeable difference.

Vibrations of the one per rev. type can usually be almost eliminated by perfect balance or track, and are definitely correctable.

Out-of-track main rotors are caused by differences in lift and drag forces or aerodynamic pitching moments on the blades. Correction used to be made after a check, consisting of a ground run with the rotor tips painted different colours and allowed to flick contact a hand-held canvas flag, which would thus be marked for colour comparison. However, this system has largely been replaced by electronic strobe systems, which are also used for the dynamic balancing of tail rotors.

Ultra-high frequency vibrations usually emanate from the engine drive shaft, tail rotor drive shaft, engine and engine fan, and are only correctable by replacement of the offending item.

The helicopter as civil transport has a firm requirement to reduce vertical vibration levels from $\pm 0.15g$ in cruising flight to $\pm 0.05g$, and modern technology has come up with some interesting solutions.

The Bell Helicopter Company has developed the Noda-Matic vibration isolation system, a concept based on the existence of node points on a vibrating beam. It involves use of a simple steel beam to which the main transmission is attached so that all main rotor vibration is impressed on the beam and produces a sine wave motion with two neutral points or nodes. When the fuselage is suspended from these nodes the main source of cabin vibration is effectively isolated. The system costs just over 2% of the helicopter gross weight.

Another development by Boeing-Vertol for the Commercial Chinook is the IRIS isolation system, which can provide a wide and very deep anti-resonant 'bucket' at any desired operating frequency by means of a spring and tuning mass between the airframe and isolated mass. The location of the 'bucket' is independent of the isolated mass and therefore remains constant as cargo loads, passenger loads or fuel loads are changed. Also the isolation system spring rate can be many times higher than that required for a conventional isolation system, thus reducing problems with static deflections under manoeuvre loads.

The IRIS system has been applied to the Commercial Chinook in two ways. Firstly, the fuel tanks have been isolated from the airframe, and since fuel weight represents one-third of this helicopter's take-off gross weight, this very large fuel mass would significantly decrease the airframe second bending mode frequency thereby increasing the basic vibration response of the total aircraft structure at the normal operating rotor r.p.m. By isolating the fuel system, the body natural frequency is made independent of the mass of fuel and the resulting vibration levels are independent of the fuel state of the aircraft. Secondly, a similar technique is applied to the cabin floor, which is a composite honeycomb as opposed to the metal floor of the military Chinook. Aircraft structural vibration is thus made independent of passenger loading, and additionally the passengers ride on an isolated cabin floor providing extremely low levels of cabin vibration.

Chapter 13

The economics of helicoptering

Helicoptering has almost militated against its own growth by virtue of its high costs. To charter a helicopter costs about two-and-a-half times that of an aeroplane of equivalent seating capacity. The reasons for this situation can be determined by the customary pattern of cost analysis, namely by considering the fixed costs, which must be absorbed regardless of utilisation, separately from running costs.

Fixed costs

Fixed costs, which are the costs arising whether or not the aircraft flies, include the following:

Equipped price including avionics – Optional extras such as flotation equipment must be included. The approximate breakdown of cost for a typical executive IFR helicopter is: engines 25%; equipped airframe 50%; radio and navaids 25%.

Depreciation – This may be taken over any period between five and ten years, but a good average is 10% over seven years down to a residual 30% of the first cost.

Insurance – This normally falls into three categories. (a) Hull coverage rates depend closely on the experience of the pilot and the type of operation to be undertaken. Such rates can vary between 2% and 10% for commercial operations and up to 15% for private operation. (b) Passenger and cargo liability is normally compulsory, and the general rules for liability reflect on the fact that air transport is an international matter as the rules are laid down in the Warsaw Convention, being ratified by the majority of countries all over the world. Many countries have, however, introduced higher domestic limits. Passenger liability will depend on the seating capacity of the aircraft. (c) Third party liability is also normally a compulsory requirement by aviation authorities to cover damage to people and property outside the aircraft.

Crew costs – These include salaries and expenses and obviously only apply to employment of professional crews.

As a general rule of thumb, the fixed annual total of depreciation and insurance costs is about one-sixth of the capital outlay for purchasing a helicopter.

Running costs

Running costs, which are the costs related to hours flown, include the following:

Fuel and oil – These prices have fluctuated considerably in the 1970s, and all the indications are that they will continue to increase substantially.

Maintenance – These are mainly labour charges and depend greatly on the maintenance schedule to which the helicopter is operated.

Spares – Allowances must be made for both scheduled and unscheduled replacement of airframe and engine parts.

Direct operating costs

The critical costs for a commercial operator are the direct operating costs, which include the running costs and some of the fixed costs reckoned on a pro rata basis of aircraft utilisation over a year. The breakdown of the direct operating costs for a medium weight helicopter used for 1000 hours per year is:

Maintenance 33%   Depreciation 20%   Fuel 17%
Insurance 12%   Crew costs 11%   Spares 7%

From the direct operating costs and average block speed, on the assumption that full use is made of the passenger seats, the seat/mile cost can be calculated. In a small five-seat helicopter with a utilisation of 600 hours per year this works out at four to five times the seat/mile cost of surface public transport.

Sikorsky S–61 Direct Operating Cost Projections

Annual costs (in 1975 dollars)	Annual hours of operation				
	1000	1500	2000	2500	3000
Total flying operation costs	$293.40	$243.60	$218.70	$203.76	$193.80
Total direct maintenance	156.43	151.42	148.08	148.08	149.75
Depreciation	314.22	209.48	157.11	125.69	104.74
Direct operating costs per hour	764.05	604.50	523.89	477.53	448.29
Direct operating costs	764050	906750	1047780	1193825	1344870
Total operating costs	1528100	1813500	2095560	2387650	2689740

Notes:
1. Source: (Sikorsky, 1974)
2. Data in 1976 dollars, but for the analysis the above costs were assumed to be in 1975 dollars.
3. The depreciation is based on a capital investment of £2.9 million, a residual value of 10%, a 15 year life, and an interest rate of 7.5%.
4. TOC assumed to be twice DOC.

Utilisation has a profound effect on direct operating costs. Halving the utilisation can nearly double the direct operating costs, therfore the primary target of the civil helicopter industry is to reduce these costs by making high utilisation a commercial practicality and so attract customers and increase profits.

Pattern of the operator industry

Strangely enough the industry does, however, benefit the customer and work against itself by being over-competitive. It has no trade agreements like the motor car industry and consequently the competitive undercutting has given a pattern to the industry, whereby there is a central core of a small number of large, expanding companies, which tend to specialise in selected areas of operations such as offshore operations, and these major operators are surrounded by a second echelon of potential growth companies with diversified tasks, and the whole surrounded by an outer ring of very small companies rising and falling with the tides of fortune.

The struggle for survival among small operators has been exacerbated in recent years by the proliferation of regulatory restrictions affecting both operators and the workforce, the complications of inflation coupled with rapidly altering international currency rates of exchange, and the tightening up of bank loans.

Key personnel

Any small operator starting up would be well advised to take a specialist management course, get himself a good accountant, lawyer, and banker and join a helicopter trade association.

A helicopter operator generally has as his only source of revenue the income produced from his operations, so every expense is vital. General costs, fixed and direct operating costs must be calculated accurately, and an accurate forecast made of annual revenue flying to determine the actual cost of operation and so establish a profit figure.

In this process an experienced chief pilot, maintenance engineer, and accountant will form a triangle of potential success. Above all, however, an all year round bread-and-butter contract should be the foundation on which any small operation is built. Without this rock the whole business may prove to be building on sand, for cash flow can only be guaranteed from such a contract basis.

A chief pilot must understand assigning and scheduling, how to formulate safety practices and compile operating manuals, keep a close check on the ability of all his pilots and study their personalities. He must always be seen to be fair and prepared to lead by example, and he should have an in-depth knowledge of regulations apertaining to his job.

A chief maintenance engineer must be able to plan maintenance activities in a way that will give maximum aircraft availability during normal revenue hours, and be flexible enough to adjust his plans to cope with sudden changes caused by unscheduled unserviceability. He must ensure good supervision of all work by low experience engineering staff, and indoctrinate them in safety procedures. He must ensure that he himself is the fount of all technical knowledge on the types of aircraft operated, and that his engineers have undertaken suitable training courses to enable them to competently carry out the work assigned to them. He must also set up a good records office to deal with the technical paperwork and to keep his staff constantly updated on regulatory changes.

In small operations the accountant is assuming an increasingly important role as taxation systems become more complex, and industrial legislation can have serious financial effects if all its implications are not fully understood. It is also of prime importance in the helicopter business to find low-interest financing for the longest possible terms while maintaining a good debt-to-equity ratio.

Of course all these people do not obviate the need for professional management, covering complete understanding of the financial, marketing, customer relations, safety, operations, and personnel sides of the business.

Statistics show that four out of every five new businesses fail within eight years, and two of these four fail within two years. This sad record is mainly due to bad management and poor marketing.

Marketing

Market research is a prerequisite of setting up any business in order to identify that the need for the product exists, and to assess the size and growth potential of that need. It means not only identifying one's customers but also one's competitors, and thus assessing one's likely share of the market. The next step is that most difficult one of pricing the product attractively yet retaining the ability to sell it at a profit. Advertising plays a powerful part in promoting sales, but nothing promotes helicopter business like a reputation for reliability and safety, and there is no cheap short-cut to these.

Advisory agencies

The pitfalls are so many in setting up in small business that countries such as the U.S.A. and the U.K. have set up government small company advisory agencies, which at no cost assist companies in identifying management problems, developing alternative solutions, and advising on marketing, accounting, product analysis and research development. The agency in the U.S.A. is the SBA (Small Business Administration), and in the U.K. the ATTITB (Air Transport and Travel Industry Training Board).

Trade associations

Trade associations such as the Helicopter Association of America and the British Helicopter Advisory Board have been set up by the industry itself as a means of communication within the industry and as a liaison body with the relevant central and local government departments. Such associations act as watchdogs for the industry's interests and monitor legislation affecting those interests. They promote helicopter operations, foster flight safety, and supply information to operators, manufacturers and customers alike.

Any small operator will find that membership of such trade associations will give him a voice in matters affecting his operations, will offer him a trouble-shooter if he has operating problems, and will give him contact with the rest of the industry. If he elects to stay aloof from such bodies he is in effect a straw in the wind of his competitors.

A different development from the normal formation of trade associations is that of the European Helicopter Association (EHA), which formed on 1 January 1981 and is a conglomerate of European nations with the aim of promoting the free flow of commercial and private helicopter traffic between European countries by the standardisation of realistic operating legislation. Unlike other trade associations the members are not individuals or companies but the national helicopter associations of each country, and these will formulate common policies in the EHA, and then pursue them individually with their own national governments, and where possible with the co-operation of the European Economic Community Transport Commission.

Chapter 14

The private helicopter

The private helicopter is so rare as to be almost an oddity, and yet some forward-looking people have predicted that it will eventually compete with or even replace the automobile. Although I believe many more helicopters will come under private ownership, I do not think these will ever reach parity with the number of commercial helicopters, far less with cars.

The dream of the everyman's helicopter has been pursued by many designers, but has always foundered on cost. In consequence the few private helicopters registered are mainly 2/3-seaters belonging to wealthy owners. This has given rise to an attitude that the helicopter is a rich man's toy and therefore not to be inflicted on the rest of the populace. This aggravating irrationality has done much to hamper the acceptance of urban heliports and so constricted commercial operations.

There is at least one home-built helicopter available on the market, but it is not certificated by the civil aviation authorities and so has very restricted operating conditions imposed on it. Such helicopters are also not popular with commercial operators, who, rightly or wrongly, feel they are unsafe and will produce an unfavourable accident rate that will reflect adversely on commercial operations.

The low-cost helicopter

It is the process of certification that has been the main deterrent to production of a low-cost helicopter, because it is both lengthy and costly. On average the American FAA takes 2–3 years to certificate a light helicopter, and the process will cost about five million U.S. dollars. This is a daunting prospect for a small company embarking on such a project, and lack of capital may drag out the whole business over ten years with the almost certain ultimate fate of foundering through lack of investment.

Up to 1980 the least expensive helicopter available sold at a price four to five times that of a comparable light aeroplane. However, the remarkable Robinson R22 two-seat helicopter has now appeared on the market at about one-third the price of the next lowest cost helicopter available, and with an operating cost similar to a light aeroplane.

It is a remarkable helicopter, because in spite of its low cost its design is not only attractive but incorporates some novel and advanced technology features, which give it high operating efficiency and environmental acceptability.

Its large diameter rotor, cambered tail rotor blades and very clean fuselage all combine to provide a fuel consumption of about 15 air miles per Imperial gallon (5 km/litre), which is equivalent to more than 20 road miles per Imperial gallon (7 km/litre). This high efficiency also gives good autorotational characteristics with a low rate of sink and shallow glide angle.

The problem of environmental acceptability has not been forgotten and in order to reduce external noise the tail rotor tip speed is low, and the transmission main drive gears have high spiral angles and tooth overlap, and the engine is fitted with a muffler. Internal noise has also been dealt with by extensive lining of the cabin with acoustical foam.

From the owner operator's point of view the main requirement is for low maintenance, and this was a primary design goal. To this end grease points have been completely eliminated by using Teflon-lined spherical and journal bearings for oscillating motion, and sealed ball bearings for rotating motion. The number of bearings required has also been reduced. The fuel system is gravity flow and does not require any fuel pumps, and there is a simplified cyclic control system eliminating many of the usual bell cranks and bearings and yet giving increased control travel and very easy entry into the helicopter. The metal rotor blades have a stainless steel leading edge along the entire length thus providing erosion protection. The clutch engagement on starting is automatic, so eliminating manual engagement which is often tricky and can be a source of trouble with amateur pilots.

Ground handling is made easy by the very low empty weight, and storage space required is minimal with the two-bladed rotor parked in the fore and aft line. In spite of its small size it has a rotor height of over eight feet (2.4 m), and this height is maintained during starting and stopping by a teeter hinge restraint, which keeps the rotor level. Such headroom clearance is a good ground safety point.

The estimated operating costs of the R22 make interesting reading and seem to substantiate its claim of being a low-cost helicopter. Costs are at 1980 prices in U.S. dollars.

Approximate initial cost (includes normal options)	$50 000
Fixed costs:	
Liability insurance ($1 000 000 single limit)	$ 1 000
Hull insurance (approx. 6% of average value: varies with use)	2 000
Fixed cost per year:	$ 3 000
Direct cost per hour:	
Depreciation (Helo retired at 3780 hours with 10% salvage value)	$ 11.90
Fuel at $1.20/U.S. gallon (80/87) and 8 g.p.h. (U.S. gallons per hour)	9.60
Oil	0.33
Reserve for periodic inspections and unscheduled maintenance	3.00
Reserve for one engine overhaul at 2000 hours ($4000 ÷ 3780)	1.06
Reserve for one aircraft overhaul at 2000 hours ($6000 ÷ 3780)	1.59
Reserve for replaced life limited components ($6077 ÷ 3780)	1.61
Direct cost per hour:	$ 29.09

Total operating cost based on 600 hours per year:

Fixed cost per flight hour:	$ 5.00
Direct cost per flight hour:	29.09
Total operating cost per hour:	$ 34.09

Total cost-per-road-mile:

Let one air mile (1.6 km) (straight line path) equal 1.5 road miles (2.4 km), and assume an average cruise speed of 105 m.p.h. (170 km/h).

$$\$34.09 \div 105 \div 1.5 = 21.6 \text{ cents/road mile (13.4 cents/road kilometre)}$$

(This total operating cost-per-mile compares favourably with some automobiles.)

This helicopter is of course piston-engined, for although the operating costs of turbine engines are lower, the capital cost of such engines are much higher – indeed prohibitively so for the private owner market. The number of R22s that could be sold could well affect the balance ratio of piston to turbine helicopters, which might have some interesting consequences. For example oil companies are not too enthusiastic about producing AVGAS (aviation gasoline), and consequently many airfields no longer stock it. General aviation might therefore welcome the boost of a large number of private helicopters to twist the arm of the aviation fuel distributors.

Private pilot training

Furthermore a host of new private helicopters means a host of new private helicopter pilots. This would give a much needed boost to flying training schools, but perhaps also provide a headache in finding sufficient instructors to cope with a sudden expansion demand.

To acquire a Private Pilot's Licence (Helicopters), the trainee must be at least seventeen years of age, medically fit, and undergo a course of both flying instruction and ground instruction, preferably at an approved flight training school. The approval of such a school by the civil aviation authorities in any country guarantees a certain standard of instruction and is usually recognised by the minimum instruction time required at such a school being shorter than at a non-approved school.

The ICAO aim is for a minimum requirement of 45 hours flight instruction at an approved flight training school, of which at least 20 hours must be dual instruction and 15 hours solo. After acquisition of the PPL(H), a pilot may further train for different type ratings on his licence, as well as a night rating.

In the initial stages of learning to fly a helicopter, fixed-wing experience may be a drawback, as the pilot finds he has an extra control to manipulate and habit dies hard. However, once the solo stage has been reached, the fixed-wing pilot's knowledge of airmanship should begin to pay dividends.

The commercial operators are not relishing the growth in the number of private helicopter pilots, as they fear that there may be an influx of 'cowboys' into the rotary-wing aerial scene, who will commit regulatory transgressions that will reflect adversely on the freedom of operation enjoyed by helicopters, particularly with regard to landing privileges.

There are therefore moves already afoot in ICAO to introduce regular proficiency checks for private pilots every thirteen months that will include both flight and ground tests as well as a recency requirement to maintain a PPL (Private Pilot's Licence) in validity.

Private helicopters of the 2/3-seat type will never be IFR certificated, so the private pilot is restricted to contact flying only. However, he will be able to acquire a night rating so a necessary part of his flying training will be basic instrument flying. This appreciation of how to be able to use flight instruments merely to maintain level flight and turn safely on to a reverse course will stand any private pilot in good stead if he or she should inadvertently run into a patch of stray cloud at night or get into goldfish bowl conditions when crossing a stretch of water. There have even been cases of loss of control when the cockpit bubble misted over suddenly in humid air conditions.

Many PPL(H) holders fly executive helicopters on business trips as well as using them partly for pleasure purposes, rather in the nature of a company car, and this makes sound economic sense from a taxation standpoint. However, a private pilot may not fly for hire or reward, so any passengers carried by such a pilot do not have the protection of public transport statutory requirements.

The private pilot never has the time to attain the proficiency standards of his professional counterpart, but since both share the same airspace there is a moral obligation on the private pilot to maintain an acceptable standard of proficiency entitling him to such sharing, and that should ideally go beyond the minimum standard demanded by civil aviation regulations if he has a pride in his status.

The question of what is a flight time minimum for real proficiency is very debatable, but many professional pilots believe that any pilot who flies less than 100 hours per year is a risk to himself and other airspace users. After all, for a private pilot that involves only two hours flying at almost every weekend in a year – not much in terms of time, but of course, quite a lot in terms of financial expense.

Chapter 15

The helicopter in sport

The tremendous flexibility in manoeuvre offered by the helicopter makes the aircraft attractive as a sporting vehicle, and its ability to carry out these various manoeuvres in a confined space gives it spectator appeal.

The Russians were the first to exploit the competitiveness of sport to enhance helicopter pilot skills. They have a large number of state subsidised flying clubs, which are in fact nurseries for military pilots in a reserve capacity. These clubs compete against each other in organised events on an area, regional, and national basis.

The events chosen for helicopter sport are mainly aimed at precision flying skills and navigational ability, although free-style events which allow originality of composition to combine with aesthetic presentation are becoming popular.

Outside Russia, the British with their love of social type sporting occasions formed the Helicopter Club of Great Britain in 1966 and so took the lead in the West. The British meetings began as rallies with tests of manoeuvring and navigational skill, and these gradually grew into Club Championships which were open to private pilots only.

The possibility of helicopter air races was raised in 1971, but the British Helicopter Advisory Board advised against such events because some helicopters can exceed Vne (speed never to be exceeded) in level flight and so impose stresses beyond design limits.

World championships

In the matter of international helicopter sport the Fédération Aéronautique Internationale (FAI), the ruling body for aviation world records and originator of the Sporting Code for all championships at national and international level, formed an International Helicopter Committee in 1956, and this led to the first Helicopter World Championships being held at Bueckeburg in the Federal Republic of Germany in 1971. These championships were limited in their scope and did not attract the Russians, but they established the framework of future events. The presence of the famous German woman pioneer helicopter pilot, Hanna Reitsch, also showed that this was a sport in which women could compete on equal terms.

In 1972 the U.K. established the British Helicopter Championships at national level, and these were open to private, commercial and military pilots of either sex.

In 1973 the U.K. organised the second Helicopter World Championships at the army aviation base at Middle Wallop, Hampshire, England, and the Russians entered a strong team, of both men and women pilots. The U.S.A. also entered both male and female competitors as did the U.K., while the Federal Republic of Germany and Austria entered military pilots only.

The five events in these Championships set the pattern for future national and world competitions. There is a Timed Arrival based on two components

Royal Air Force Whirlwind competing in Second Helicopter World Championships

– time overhead target at 500 feet (150 m) altitude after flying a minimum distance of 15 miles (24 km), followed by time of arrival after completing a 3½ minute landing circuit from the overhead position. Penalty points are given for seconds early or late at the overhead and arrival gates, and for any obvious change of attitude to lose or gain time in the terminal phases of the exercise. There is also a Navigation Event involving flight planning, land-mark identification, and cruise speed control. In both these events the crewman plays a vital part.

The next two events are aimed at testing the manoeuvring skill of the helicopter pilot under the direction of his crewman. The Precision Event can take various forms but the most popular with crews and spectators alike is weaving an underslung bucket of pre-weighed water through a slalom course of 10-foot (3-metre) high poles forming gates, and finally placing it on a ringed target. Penalty points are given for excessive time taken, weight of water spilled, and distance from target centre. Bonus points are given for time taken less than standard.

The Rescue Event involves some aspect of rescue operations such as lowering a bucket of water through the small window in a sloping roof on to a ringed target inside the structure. Penalty and bonus points are generally as for the Precision Event.

The Free-style Event is a three minute display of individual pilot skill and is aimed at combining artistic flair with ability to fly the helicopter to its limits. The pilot must have submitted his programme to a panel of judges, who decide whether it is safe in the light of the pilot's experience and the aircraft's known flight characteristics.

The advent of the semi-rigid rotor has given the helicopter the ability to loop and roll, so the spectator appeal of this event is very considerable.

The second Helicopter World Championships also initiated team events, with each participating country nominating three crews, whose collective points give the team tally, but the points would only score in four events, as the free-style event is considered an individualistic competition.

The third Helicopter World Champtionships were not held until 1978 at Vitebsk in Russia, the gap in the planned two year sequence being caused by the world energy crisis in 1974 and its subsequent repercussions.

These championships were attended by three Western countries and three from the Communist bloc. They followed the pattern of the previous world championships and were again highly successful, attracting a huge crowd of 200 000 to the opening ceremony.

There will again be an extra time gap before the fourth World Champion-ships in Poland in 1981, because of the Olympic Games occurring in 1980.

There is every indication that these world championships will grow and encourage the growth of national clubs and national champtionships. The U.S.A. formed the Helicopter Club of America in 1979 and others will undoubtedly follow.

Future prospects

Perhaps the biggest fillip to helicopter sport will be the advent of the small, inexpensive but certificated helicopter such as the Robinson R22. This would help to overcome the main drawback to private pilot entry into major championships, namely the cost of training for the events. It is of course this aspect that gives the military pilot such an advantage, but championships' organisers have tried to even this out by giving only a month's notice of the details of the events, so that practice time is limited to this period for all potential competitors.

In anticipation of the growth of helicopter sport, the International Helicopter Committee of the FAI has established a list of international judges, who are considered competent to officiate at events of international status.

Chapter 16

The growing helicopter market

There is every evidence that the future outlook for the civil helicopter industry is indeed bright. Market predictions from all sources are of growth of a significant order in the next decade (1980–90).

The industry has a history of steady growth recorded in all user countries, rising to a peak of 60% in the early 1970s. Although this rate was slowed by the energy crisis of 1974, it recovered to a more stable rate of just over 15%. This has meant that civil helicopter fleets in such countries as the U.S.A., Canada and the U.K. have virtually doubled in the period 1975–80, and statistics seem to indicate that commercial operators increased at about half this rate.

The first big milestone in helicopter usage came on the military side in the early 1960s when the number of rotary-wing aircraft procured by the U.S. military exceeded the number of fixed-wing aircraft. The second big mile-stone looks like occurring in 1985, when the number of civil helicopters in use in the world should exceed the number of military rotary-wing aircraft.

Ten-year forecast

The generally accepted forecast is that 25 000 helicopters will be built in the 1980s, and that 15 000 of these will be civil and 10 000 military. A lucrative civil market therefore lies ahead for helicopter manufacturers and competition will be fierce, especially between American and European companies.

In 1980 helicopters made up half of the military, 20% of general aviation, and 5% of the overall commercial aircraft markets. The civil helicopter market was worth two billion U.S. dollars, and six major U.S. manufacturers (Bell, Boeing-Vertol, Enstrom, Hiller, Hughes, Sikorsky) together with four European (Aerospatiale of France, Agusta of Italy, Messerschmitt-Bolkow-Blohm of Germany, Westland of U.K.) are the main contenders for this and future prizes.

World markets

The major markets are the United States and Canada, Europe and Latin America, with the Far East, Middle East and Africa growing in importance. The 1980 geographical distribution of civil helicopters and the expected growth in these areas is:

61.1% in North and South America will grow by 15% per year

17.3% in Europe (excluding Communist bloc) will grow by 10% per year
17.1% in Far East will grow by 15% per year
 4.5% in Middle East and Africa will grow by 12½% per year.

The U.S.A. had a very firm grip on the helicopter manufacturing industry up till 1976, when 84% of the 28 000 helicopters built up to that time were of American design, but the pattern began to change in 1977 when the European designs began to make a real impact, and it is now predicted that of the 15 000 helicopters likely to be built between 1977 and 1983, the Europeans will have designed 38%. Since the U.S. manufacturers of civil helicopters depend heavily on the export market in terms of both number of units sold and dollar volume of such sales, they must look on the European competition with some apprehension, especially as Europe has been the primary export market for civil helicopters.

The early American dominance was helped by the chaos in Europe at the end of World War II, but then Europe began to build up its industry based on U.S. licensing agreements together with a major effort at innovative design. The latter asset has given Europe its marketing breakthrough to a strong exporting position.

The scale of the licensing agreement between Westland and Sikorsky can be gauged from the fact that Westland built 133 Dragonflies (Sikorsky S–51), 416 Whirlwinds (S–55), 352 Wessex (S–58), 170 Sea Kings (S–61) and 36 Commando variants by the end of 1979, with a further 20 Sea Kings and 13 Commandoes on order.

On the technological side Aerospatiale in conjunction with Turbomeca introduced gas turbine power to rotorcraft in the Alouette 2, while MBB pioneered fibreglass rotor blades leading to the semi-rigid rotor of the Bo. 105 and the rigid rotor of the Westland Lynx. Aerospatiale also developed the shrouded tail rotor known as the fenestron on the Gazelle and Dauphin helicopters.

Europe has been helped in the development of its helicopter industry in the 1970s by the American commitment in Vietnam, when the enormous demand for military helicopters caused the U.S. industry to concentrate on mass production and neglect export and innovation. Another big helping hand came from the European engine industry spurred by France's Turbomeca developing small gas turbines in the early 1950s, followed in this specialist field by the U.K.'s Rolls-Royce Company.

Forecast usage

Of the 15 000 civil helicopters predicted to be required in the decade 1980–90 the following is the estimated breakdown:

63% in aerial work, which covers such activities as crop spraying, power line inspection, police work, filming and T.V. coverage, etc. This growth will be largely due to expanding use of helicopters in emerging countries, particularly in agricultural aviation to feed an expanding world population. There will also be an increasing requirement for heavy lift crane helicopters to aid construction work in the development of countries with large expanses of terrain inaccessible to or difficult for surface transport.

22% in offshore support operations. There were in 1980 some 300 oil rigs in the world and this is likely to increase to 700 by 1985. Already 25 000 people per week are being moved on this type of work, and daily there are 2000 movements in the North Sea alone made by twin-engine helicopters, which offer both safety and all-weather capability in such an unfriendly environment.

10% as air taxis or scheduled public transport. The helicopter charter business has for long been the backbone of the industry, but is being overtaken by the other commercial sectors of helicoptering. Scheduled services have generally not flourished in the past, but this has been mainly due to lack of a viable helicopter for the task, and is now likely to change with the advent of larger machines capable of carrying at least 40 passengers.

5% as executive transport. This figure can be misleading, until it is remembered that such helicopters are largely confined to the more sophisticated business countries, e.g. executive or company helicopters make up 17% of the U.K. total. The successful company executive is a high-salaried individual, whose valuable time is often ill spent on congested roads or inadequate railway systems. As the helicopter normally has a better door to door time than the aeroplane over distances up to 250 miles (400 km), it becomes commercially attractive to the business executive. New executive helicopters are speedier and so open up the competitive range to 400 miles (640 km). They are also quieter and more comfortable and many offer twin-engine safety and all-weather capability.

Private helicoptering has not been included in this analysis, because it still represents a very small fraction of the world helicopter content, and is likely to remain so until a reasonably low-priced, small, reliable and certificated machine appears on the market, such as the Robinson R22. Its impact will be able to be gauged by about 1982 when it should be operating world-wide.

The demand will overall be mainly for light and medium weight machines, and this again will help the European manufacturers, whose know-how lies mainly in these classes. In the U.S.A. there may be various mergers of companies until by 1990 there are only two major manufacturers, one specialising in light and medium weight helicopters, the other in large machines, but if this happens a similar rationalisation seems inevitable in Europe.

Chapter 17

Technological progress in helicopter development

Helicoptering, while not in its infancy, is certainly still in its youth from a technological development standpoint, and this has bedevilled its progress, particularly with regard to public acceptance of the helicopter as a modern mode of transport. The areas that concern the public are safety, performance, and costs, and these of course are the same areas that concern the operator.

The helicopters of the 1950s suffered 50 major accidents per 100 000 flight hours, but by the 1970s the introduction of the turbine engine had reduced this figure to 10 per 100 000 hours. This increase in safety was of course not solely due to the engine situation but also to the lessons learned about aeroelasticity and structural dynamics from the first generation of piston-engine helicopters. However, the fundamental change of engine design pointed the way ahead by reducing the number of moving parts that can fail, and the helicopter has always had many more moving parts than its fixed-wing counterpart.

Apart from the engine, the major moving part areas of the helicopter are the main rotor, the tail rotor, and the transmission system. In every one of these areas strenuous technological development is going on aimed at increasing reliability and performance and reducing direct operating costs.

Main rotor systems

The most common rotor system in use in the 1970s has been the fully articulated rotor, but the rigid rotor and its modified forms are gaining in use, for it increases stability, reduces vibration, and improves handling. Elastomeric bearings have been developed to accomplish all the blade movements, but the bearlingless main rotor (BMR) has now been flown without any mechanical articulation at all. The BMR offers four main advantages – lower blade weight by eliminating the feathering bearings, lower hub weight, reduced cost of maintenance and manufacturing because of simplicity, and reduced hub drag because of lower profile.

In the experimental stage is the circulation control rotor, which has air pumped from the hub plenum chamber through slots at the trailing edge of the blades, and can achieve trimmed flight with no moving parts other than the blades as well as giving a high lift coefficient.

The controlled twist rotor, also in the experimental stage, redistributes airloads on the blade surface by having torsionally soft blades, which are twisted by conventional pitch horn links inboard and control flaps at the outboard end.

The use of composite materials in blade design has made great advances from the early designs combining a metal spar with a fibreglass body and bonded with polyester resins, which were not reliable enough to guarantee safe operation. However, with the development of the superior bonding epoxy resins, fibreglass blades now offer infinite life, better performance in lift, speed, and fuel consumption, lower maintenance costs, improved noise and vibration characteristics.

The extent of the performance gains is illustrated by a direct comparison between production models of the Aerospatiale Puma fitted with both metal and fibreglass blades. The fibreglass equipped version gave an increase in maximum gross weight of 6¼% with no increase in power; was 17½ knots (32½ km/h) faster at identical maximum gross weights and power settings; had a 5% lower fuel consumption at maximum gross weight.

These performance gains arise from the fact that blade weight on a helicopter type cannot be lightened without adversely affecting autorotation criteria, so since fibreglass is lighter than metal the design of the composite blade can be longer and wider to provide better performance.

Due to the infinite life of fibreglass blades, the blade maintenance costs are decreased to at least one-third of those of metal blades, and the lower vibration level of the fibreglass blades coupled with stress reduction has effectively lengthened the fatigue life of many other components. The strength of the blades is also shown by the fact that induced charges of lightning have not penetrated the blade, but harmlessly run along the metal covering of the leading edge.

Any separation in bonding can be repaired simply by drilling a small hole in the blade and injecting epoxy through a syringe. There are also no problems with notches, scores, fatigue, or corrosion.

The improvments in noise and vibration also affect passenger comfort and the public acceptance of the helicopter to a marked degree.

Rotor technology has only increased hovering efficiency from 70% to 75% in some forty years, but a breakthrough has been made with composite materials, which should show an increase to 85% by the mid-1980s.

During the 1960s and 1970s helicopter payloads have increased fourfold, and the payload to gross weight ratio has increased from one-third to one-half, and composite materials could improve this to two-thirds.

Maximum speeds have increased by 120 m.p.h. (190 km/h) to over 200 m.p.h. (320 km/h) in the same period, with similar improvement in cruise speeds. Generally designers only installed enough power in helicopters to meet the hovering mission requirement. In comparison to fixed-wing aircraft this is a relatively low power level and does not permit high speed when drag reduction is neglected as it has been so glaringly in rotary-wing aircraft.

The helicopters of the 1980s have retractable landing gear, low drag rotor hubs, and streamlined fuselage shapes which are moving them towards the 200 knots (370 km/h) speed mark.

Transmission systems

Over 30% of the direct maintenance costs of helicopters are created by transmissions. Intensive research is underway to develop transmissions that will be installed in the factory and stay in for the life of the airframe, using new high temperature gear and bearing materials, lubricants, fail-safe components and composite case structure. This could result in a 75% life cycle cost saving.

New high-hot hardness steels provide more than 30% increase in surface load capacity for critical gears, and substantial improvement in scuffing resistance compared to previous gear materials. High-speed tapered roller bearings can carry heavier radial and thrust loads per pound of weight than any other type of bearing, thus allowing operations at speeds more than double the limit for standard bearings. High contact ratio gears redistribute the tooth load so that the teeth can carry more load with no increase in stress, and such gearing provides some of the benefits of helical gearing, like higher load sharing and lower noise, without the assembly and thrust problems of helical gears.

The use of planetary gear boxes is decreasing, and since the normal planetary gear box uses a large number of gears, the consequent reduction will result in lower total costs and increased reliability.

Tail rotor systems

The use of fewer bearings and bearing supports in tail rotor drive shafts results in lower maintenance requirements, and the use of viscous damped drive shaft supports reduces vibration in this area. Composite materials can be employed in the tail rotors themselves, and the tendency is for the latter to become bearingless. Such a tail rotor is not only lighter but has 30% fewer parts than conventional tail rotor systems.

On-condition maintenance

Increasing the annual utilisation of a helicopter will reduce the operating cost on a pro rata basis, but high utilisation requires a reduction in maintenance time and an extension in life of the system.

In the gas turbine field, examination of components by methods such as the spectograph oil analysis programme has led to a rapid increase in time between overhauls, a reduction in premature removals, and a reduction in flight shutdowns. However, the system suffers from differential sensitivity in that it can readily detect wear failures, but has difficulty with fatigue type failures.

The philosophy of condition monitoring is the real answer to increasing utilisation in helicopter operations and a prime example of this has been the magnetic chip detector in both gas turbines and transmissions.

Vibration is the destructive force at the heart of helicopter unserviceability. Its detection and elimination by vibration analysis is the most hopeful area of condition monitoring, but the technique will require the learning time to be reduced to instant interpretation.

The blade inspection method (BIM), whereby rotor blades have a section of the aerofoil pressurised so that any leakage is indicative of crack detection or early warning of spar deterioration, can be cockpit monitored and will permit on-condition blade overhaul without a mandatory retirement time.

With these systems of fault-finding, the time-lifing of components will be replaced by an on-condition criterion, which will drastically reduce maintenance costs by cutting maintenance man hours per flight hour. Already the ratio has decreased in the twenty years of the 1960s and 1970s from 25:1 to 3:1, and this should reach better than 0.5:1.

Flight control systems

In the realm of helicopter flight safety, material failures account for only 30% of the total accidents, while basic pilot error contribute 65%. The application of fly-by-wire in place of mechanical push-pull rods and cables and pulleys is a breakthrough in helicopter flight control systems. When this technology is complemented by responsive rotor systems designed to produce in harmony the forces and moments that control the helicopter, then the pilot will have as stable and controllable a vehicle as a fixed-wing aeroplane.

Crashworthiness

On the assumption that accidents will never be totally eliminated in helicopter flying, there is much that technology can do to minimise the effects of a crash. Designing for survivability must, however, be a matter of compromise in the commercial field. For example the distinctive egg-shaped fuselage of the Hughes 500 helicopter has demonstrated a remarkable ability to remain relatively intact in serious crashes, yet the passenger cabin is often criticised as claustrophobic.

Crash avoidance, as it has sometimes been termed, can be built into a helicopter by expanded operating tolerances, reserve power, fault monitoring devices, fail-safe systems, and improved autorotation capabilities.

The survivability aspect of crash safety is mainly concentrated on crew and passenger protection. The U.S. Army has set an impact velocity of 42 ft/s (12.8 m/s) as the safe-crash criteria in post-1980 helicopters. This is equivalent to saying that the crew should be able to walk away from a 30 m.p.h. (48 km/h) car crash. Much of this crew protection is provided by the combination of energy absorbing landing gear, crushable fuselage structure, seat and safety-harness design, and protection against post-crash fires.

However, there is still the problem of the rotor breaking loose on impact and injuring the occupants. Since the rotor of a light turbine helicopter at its normal r.p.m. has the kinetic energy of a car travelling at 60 m.p.h. (96 km/h) it has to be restrained during a crash.

Vibration

At the other end of the scale, technology applies itself to crew and passenger comfort in the matter of vibration, which is probably the most disturbing characteristic to commercial passengers. Again the U.S. Army is setting the trend by demanding vibration levels below $0.05g$ in their post-1980 helicopters.

Vibration can be attacked at the rotor hub by bifilar absorbers, which incorporate a linkage that counteracts the rotor system excitation before it reaches the airframe. Alternatively an anti-resonance isolation system has been developed, which can be applied to rotor or fuel tank systems, but has its greatest potential in application to the cabin floor so that passengers are in effect afloat in the main fuselage.

Breakthrough

Helicopter technology can therefore be seen to be at a rapidly progressive stage, which puts rotary-wing development into a phase comparable to fixed-wing development some forty-five years before. However, unlike the fixed-wing technology of those days when a breakthrough was looked for in performance and found in wing sweepback, rotary-wing development seeks a breakthrough in transmission technology as its most pressing need.

Just such a breakthrough is around the corner if the research being carried out by the U.S. National Aeronautics and Space Agency on Multiroller Traction Drive comes to full fruition. The system utilises smooth metal rollers arranged in a planetary system, but unlike toothed gear drives the rollers do not touch one another but are separated by a miniscule film of lubricant.

Development of the roller drives has been underway for over ten years and should enter the realms of in-service practability in the mid-1980s. They offer a number of advantages of outstanding merit:

(a) Quiet, almost vibrationless means of transmitting power.
(b) Simpler and less expensive to manufacture than helical or planetary gears.
(c) Lighter and smaller than conventional gear boxes.
(d) As efficient as toothed gear systems.
(e) Higher reliability and are less susceptible to breakdown and wear than conventional gear boxes.

With this exciting technological prospect ahead, together with the whole on-condition maintenance philosophy now pervading the rotary-wing scene, it seems inevitable that the operator is in for a more productive time and the customer for a safer, more comfortable, and cheaper helicopter ride.

Chapter 18

The future outlook for the helicopter

A look into the crystal ball for prognostications of the helicopter's future in the next decade shows a reasonably clear picture, which begins to cloud over a little when one probes deeper towards the last decade of the twentieth century. Not that there is any real doubt that the helicopter will still be with us in 2000, but the question is in what form.

The way ahead in the 1990s has been largely clarified by the research and development budget passed by the U.S. Congress in 1978, from which stemmed the Rotorcraft Task Force created by the National Aeronautics and Space Agency (NASA) to assess the state of helicopter technology, determine needs, and develop a research programme for the future development of advanced civil and military rotorcraft.

NASA research programme

In its Task Force Report on Advanced Rotorcraft Technology dated 15 October 1978, NASA proposed a 398 million U.S. dollar, ten-year research programme, with eight goals:

1. *Noise reduction.* Limit noise footprints outside heliport boundaries to 85 EPNdB.
2. *Vibration reduction.* Reduce current vibration levels to 0.01–0.05g.
3. *Reliability and maintainability.* Improve by a factor of 3.
4. *All-weather capability.* Less than 1% time loss due to weather conditions.
5. *Safety improvements.* Fivefold reduction in accident rate.
6. *Flying qualities.* Provide passengers with equivalent 'jet smooth' aeroplane ride.
7. *Productivity improvement.* Achieve higher speeds and greater payloads.
8. *Reduced fuel consumption.* Fuel savings of 20% while increasing range and endurance.

In the quest for these goals the Task Force 'identified' four major programme elements: (a) aerodynamics and structures (b) propulsion (c) flight control and avionic systems (d) vehicle configurations.

(A) Aerodynamics and structures

The focus is on three areas: acoustics, vibration, and composites. The goal is to develop a method for future helicopter design that reduces external noise by 5–10 dB, improves hover efficiency by 10%, and improves cruise efficiency by 20%. A substantial reduction of airframe vibration and internal noise is sought, together with the extension of hub/rotor technology to produce designs with two-thirds fewer parts, 10% to 15% less cost, infinite life, and 10% to 15% less weight. On the structures side the objective is to extend the application of composite materials to the helicopter airframe, thus reducing structural weight and so improving payload capability, while at the same time enhancing damage tolerance and fatigue life.

(B) Propulsion

The main objectives in this area are to improve engine and power transfer reliability and maintainability, reduce engine fuel consumption at cruise power, improve environmental acceptability, and reduce manufacturing and operating costs.

Because of the relatively small size of helicopter gas turbine engines, performance improvements are difficult to achieve. Also current analytical design techniques are not adequate for accurately predicting the performance characteristics of small turbine-engine components.

High operating costs of current helicopters are largely due to the maintenance rate of the transmission components, so much of the propulsion programme is aimed at improving future rotorcraft transmissions and other power transfer components as well as reducing the size, weight, noise, vibration, and cost of these components. New advanced concepts such as traction drive/planetary gear combinations, variable speed, and convertible drive designs will be explored.

(C) Flight control and avionic systems

The overall objective of this programme is to develop the technology to significantly enhance the unique operating capabilities of advanced rotorcraft, with the emphasis on all-weather operations and active control technology. The all-weather systems programme is aimed at developing operating techniques needed for safe instrument flight operations for remote sites and high density terminal areas. For remote sites the goal is to provide IMC (Instrument Meteorological Conditions) capability down to decision heights as low as 100 feet (30 m). For high density terminal operations, the goal is to provide IMC capability down to decision heights less than 50 feet (15 m), using terminal areas' navigation and guidance aids.

Active control technology offers improvement in performance factors such as fuel efficiency, manoeuvrability, handling qualities and precision flight path control, potential reaction of control surfaces, the elimination of vehicle empennage, and the reduction of weight and complexity. The programme will focus on two major task areas:

(i) Full Authority Systems Technology will emphasise the design, evaluation, and validation of flight critical, full authority systems concepts typically associated with fly-by-wire, fly-by-light, and control configured vehicle technology.

(ii) Mission Capability Improvements will focus on the design and validation of high precision, low altitude, fast response guidance, and navigation system technology. In this respect the Global Positioning System holds great promise. It is based on a network of satellites that broadcast high quality signals to earth. Coverage will be complete and accurate regardless of altitude or terrain.

(D) Vehicle configurations

The main helicopter configuration is the single large overhead rotor containing two to five blades and a small tail rotor as perfected by Igor Sikorsky. Next in popularity is the tandem rotor layout such as employed in the Chinook, and which offers three main advantages – a large centre of gravity range, hover capability unaffected by wind direction, and freedom from the vortex ring state effects.

Other configurations such as the biaxial (twin rotor) concept, the inter-meshing (syncropter) concept, the coaxial, and the rotor tip jet concept have been tried with varying degrees of success, but none has made the top production grade.

The Chinook demonstrates the wide CG range permissible with the tandem rotor configuration

All indications are that in the late 1980s and early 1990s users will demand advanced vehicle configurations with high speed, large cargo and heavy external lift capabilities.

Because there are increasing indications that speed will return as an important factor in selected civil and military missions, high speed investigations are aimed at assessing the high speed potential of new aircraft concepts such as the X-wing, tilt rotor, ABC, and winged compound. This will be the first focal point of the Vehicle Configuration Programme, while the second will focus on the large rotorcraft concept, aimed at developing and evaluating technology for cargo, transport, and heavy lift applications involving the study of conventional vehicles as well as the tilt rotor concept, the quad rotor concept, both tilting and non-tilting, and the multi-lift concept.

There is little doubt that the catalyst for the NASA programme is the concern that American rotorcraft technology is in danger of losing its lead to its European competitors. The seriousness of this situation for American manufacturers was emphasised in 1979 when the U.S. Coast Guards chose the French SA–366 Dauphin for its Short Range Recovery (SRR) helicopter programme in preference to the home product offered.

There has been virtually a new generation of helicopter each decade from 1950 onwards and the fourth generation is now in the experimental stage. Some of these experiments are revolutionary in concept and exciting in performance. A brief study of three of these experimental helicopters is well worth-while here.

(a) *ABC (Advancing Blade Concept)*. First flown in 1973, it is a unique rotary-wing vehicle that combines the advantages of a low-speed helicopter with those of a high-speed aircraft. It has two counter-rotating coaxial main rotors, and thus does not require a tail rotor. Directional control is accomplished by differential collective pitch on the rotors at low speeds, controlled by the rudder pedals, and gradually phased out until at 80 knots (148 km/h) the aeroplane type rudders take over.

Sikorsky ABC experimental helicopter

The rotor blades are rigidly mounted to the rotor hubs with pitch change bearings similar to a propeller. At high speed the retreating blades are unloaded and the majority of the rotor load is carried on the advancing blades of both rotors. This eliminates stall on the retreating blade and allows the helicopter to achieve unprecedented speed and manoeuvrability.

The advantages of the ABC over the conventional helicopter are that rotor lift can be maintained, and actually increased, with increasing forward speed; and that high speed can be maintained at high altitudes. Longer ranges and higher speeds at maximum lift-to-drag ratios are the result. The ABC also generates significantly less noise than the conventional helicopter. Powered by two jet engines and two auxiliary propulsion units it is designed by Sikorsky to achieve a maximum speed of over 300 knots (555 km/h).

(b) *X-wing*. In this Lockheed helicopter the X-wing rotates as a normal rotor for vertical take-off, and once airborne will lock in place to form a stationary wing for forward flight, thus making high speeds possible as in an aeroplane.

(c) *Tilt rotor*. The Bell XV–15 has two three-blade rotors on an engine pod at each extremity of its high wing layout. For vertical take-off the pods are in the vertical plane, and then they are rotated to translate to forward flight until at high speed the aircraft in effect becomes a turbo-prop aeroplane.

Bell XV–15 tilt rotor research aircraft

Engine design

In parallel with helicopter design has been engine design, and now the fourth generation jet engines are continuing the trend of turbo-shaft technology in the direction of increased engine pressure ratio and temperature in the quest for cost-effectiveness.

Specific Fuel Consumption (SFC) is the practical measure of efficiency. The specific power is the ratio of output power to quantity of airflow through the engine, and airflow establishes the size, weight and volume of the engine and therefore correlates with its cost.

Pressure ratios of 20 to 1 are certain in the 1980s, and temperatures of over 2400°F (1315°C) because of improved technology of turbine cooling in addition to metallurgical development. However, the rate at which SFC can be further reduced without departing from the simple turbo-shaft cycle is diminishing because of the fundamental thermodynamic characteristics, so designers will have to utilise variable turbine geometry, variable cooling techniques, recouperative and regenerative cycles, and new engine rating techniques.

Engine operating life has increased and seems to be approaching a practical limit where an engine utilised for 400 hours per year, will have an expected service life of 15 years. Engine maintenance has dropped by 75% cost per engine flight hour in three generations of turbo-jets, and is likely to achieve less than ten U.S. dollars per hour in fourth generation engines. With maintenance costs reduced so dramatically, the rising cost of fuel begins to assume a new importance in engine operating costs, so the emphasis in future will be on further SFC reductions.

A far look ahead

A look into the 1990s involves more nebulous predictions, but it seems likely that most of the jobs being done by helicopters will be of a new nature, and that material and energy shortages will have considerable influence on airframe and engine design. Regulatory controls on noise and performance requirements will also have their effects on design. Certainly development costs will have quadrupled in the year 2000 in comparison with such costs fifty years earlier.

Materials will play a major role in the structural designs of the 1990s, particularly composites with their offers of substantial weight reductions, improved strength, and greater reliability. There will be many other material advancements such as ceramic type bearings, transmission cases made from metal matrix composites, short fibres (whiskers) technology where nearly perfect crystalline structures of carbon give a specific strength 50 times that of steel.

Engines and their accessories with their high degree of sophistication cause the major portion of material failures in helicopters, so they will have to be simplified in the 1990s. This change may be forced on engine designers by the introduction of alternative fuels, which will also resize and redistribute fuel tankage.

The efficiency of forward flight as measured by lift/drag ratio (L/D) has advanced from less than four in early helicopters to about five in the 1980s, and should reach values of up to eight in the 1990s. With the improvements in L/D, best range cruise speeds will increase by some 15%.

The helicopter's inherent speed limitations due to compressibility on the advancing rotor blade, stall on the retreating blade, and the high drag of the exposed rotor hub are best tackled by radical changes in configuration, and of these the tilt rotor concept seems the only one that might produce speeds of 400 m.p.h. (640 km/h) in the 1990s.

On the piloting side, the use of simulators for training will grow enormously and should reduce accident rates and insurance rates. Cockpit computers will monitor all the helicopter's vital signs and warn of impending problems or provide corrective action.

Onboard computers will also navigate, assist with communications, be capable of flying, hovering, and landing the rotorcraft automatically. This technique will also be applied to remote piloted helicopters being developed for military surveillance duties, but it is difficult to foresee a cost-effective application for such devices to commercial operations.

In essence, the future of the helicopter seems assured at least to the end of the twentieth century, and it will almost certainly continue to flourish in commercial use well beyond that but in forms that may be as different from Igor Sikorsky's VS–300 of 1939 as is Concorde from the DC–3.

Mankind already owes a great debt to the helicopter in the field of rescue, oil support operations, and agriculture, and that list of superb achievement will inevitably grow as the helicopter develops its full potential as a workhorse for the advancement of human progress.

Chapter 19

The other side of the fence

In 1978, I had the good fortune to visit Russia for the third Helicopter World Championships and meet Russian helicopter pilots and designers, as well as to examine and fly in the Russian machines.

It soon becomes apparent that Russian helicopter design and operation are based on a different philosophy from that of the Western World. There is no commercial competition, so the Soviet designers aim for simplicity, functional efficiency, and ease of production.

There is a basic ruggedness about Russian helicopters that immediately strikes the eye. They lack smoothness of finish and elegance of line, but they are built to operate in the extremes of the vast agricultural arena of the steppes in summer and the Siberian wilderness in winter.

This ruggedness is evidenced by the fact that Soviet helicopters are some 5% to 10% heavier than their Western counterparts, and this largely stems from the labour-intensive approach of the U.S.S.R., which has a large pool of craftsmen available at low cost.

The production runs of Soviet helicopters are also longer than those in the West, being based on a minimum of five years, and this has a profound effect on costs in favour of the Russians.

All Soviet helicopter designs are in essence military, and when operated in a commercial role they are derated to some 70% to 80% of their available power, but in spite of that have much shorter TBOs (Times Between Overhauls) than Western designs. The overall view that military machines have short lives, and so long-term reliability is not of paramount importance. If costs are kept low, replacement takes on a different significance.

To fly a Russian helicopter is to feel one has stepped back some ten years in technology, for the vibration and noise levels are high, speeds are lower, and there is a feeling of brute force with little finesse. However, the Russians ably demonstrated in competition that finesse lies largely in the hands of the pilot.

One of the awe-inspiring sights is to see a line-up of old Mi–1 helicopters start up with their compressed air kicking the engine into furious rotation with clouds of blue smoke. Brutal, but designed to breathe life into frozen engines in a Russian winter. With treatment like that, engine life is likely to be strictly limited, but then replacement is cheap.

To inquire about safety records in Russia is to invite an abrupt lowering of the Iron Curtain, so diplomacy is to be exercised in this area. Maybe ignorance is bliss.

Commercial helicoptering on a free enterprise basis does not exist in the Soviet Union, where the passenger and cargo helicopters are operated by the state airline Aeroflot, and the aerial work machines, mainly crop-spraying and heavy lift are operated on a para-military basis by regional authorities. This arrangement at least ensures less intervention from environmentalists, although Russian authorities are not oblivious to the preservation of the environment.

Russian Kamov Ka. 26 utility helicopter

Certainly there are large numbers of helicopters to be seen engaged in agricultural fertilisation, and there is little doubt that the Russians have acquired a lot of expertise in this field. This is illustrated by the design of the Kamov Ka. 26, which employs the flying chassis concept permitting the use of quickly-removable equipment to cater for various duties such as spraying of liquid chemicals or dusting with dry chemicals, or alternatively fit a cargo tray or passenger cabin. In the latter capacity it is hardly in the luxury class, but then if you want to get to Siberia the easy way in winter you are unlikely to complain when you consider the alternatives. This little helicopter is certainly unique in being a twin piston-engine machine with coaxial rotors, a twin boom fuselage, and four-leg undercarriage, all of which create so much drag that it cruises at only 85 m.p.h. (137 km/h), and although that speed may not be very exciting for public transport work, it is more than adequate for spraying or dusting.

The Soviet Union has operated helicopter scheduled passenger services since late 1958, when the Mi–4, a single-engine 12-seat machine appeared on the Simferopol-Yalta service in the Crimea. This route is a classic case of the 'no attractive alternative mode of transport' syndrome, because the Black Sea resort of Yalta is screened by a range of mountains immediately behind the town up to a height of some 6000 ft (1800 m). The nearest airport at Simferopol is about 25 miles (40 km) inland and the surface connection to Yalta is a tortuous mountain road necessitating a journey of 2½ to 3 hours. The helicopter route, although not direct in order to avoid high ground, is about ½ hour. Similar helicopter services connect the Black Sea resorts of Alder, Gagra, Khosta, Lazerevskaya and Gelendzhik, with the inland airport at Sochi.

On 20 July 1980, Mi–4s began operating services between Moscow Central Air Terminal and Sheremetyevo Airport, and on 1 November 1960 began linking Bykovo and Vnukovo Airports with Moscow and with each other. Later on the new Domodedovo Airport was similarly connected to the city centre by a helicopter service.

From these beginnings, the U.S.S.R. now has a vast network of helicopter scheduled services, mainly utilising twin turbine-engine machines such as the 28 passenger Mi–8. However, the Russians have pioneered very large helicopters and the Mi–6 has the capacity to carry 75 passengers.

The twin-engine Mi–6 is a vast helicopter with a five-blade main rotor, each blade of which is 55 ft 9¼ in (16.999 m) long. It first flew in 1957, being produced to a specification for a heavy lift vehicle, and is extensively used on construction work throughout the country. Later versions of the Mi–6 were fitted with a small wing which off-loaded the rotor by about 20% in cruising flight. This wing could be readily detached for lifting operations.

A variant of the Mi–6 was the Mi–10, which appeared in 1960 with a huge stalky quadricycle undercarriage to give maximum clearance when straddling bulky cargo loads. This was followed in 1966 by the Mi–10K with much shorter undercarriage legs and with a rearward-facing pilot control cabin beneath the nose after the style of the Sikorsky Skycrane and for the same purpose of precise positioning of external loads. These variants were preludes to the mighty, experimental Mi–V.12 described in the next chapter.

One aspect where the Russian helicopters show their origin is that of airframe anti-icing equipment, which is standard fit to all their machines. This varies from the Ka. 26 system which supplies de-icing fluid into the rotor blades, to the electrical anti-icing system heating the main and tail rotors and windshields of the Mi–8. The latter system is actuated automatically by an ice detector, or can be switched on manually, allowing the Mi–8 to operate in sea level temperatures of 5°F (− 15°C) or possibly lower.

The Russians have granted the Polish state helicopter industry, Pezetel of Swidnik, the licence to build and indeed export some of their designs. Such a

Polish built version of Russian Mi–2 on forestration spraying duty

design, the Mi–2, is being marketed in the U.S.A. with American engines and avionics.

From the Western standpoint Russian export helicopters are attractively cheap in price, but their old-fashioned looks and the doubts about their reliability may militate against their marketing success.

The Poles use their home produced Mil helicopters mainly on agricultural work and air ambulance services. In the latter role the Ministry of Health employs thirty Mi–2s dispersed at thirteen bases and these make 20 000 flights per year.

For agricultural work the Poles set up a special state enterprise in 1975, and called it ZEUS for short. This company now operates over fifty helicopters from 31 bases in Poland and 3 abroad – Egypt, Nigeria and the Sudan, treating 3 million acres in all. In the past they have also operated in Iran, Iraq, Libya and Bulgaria, but after the purchase of Mi–2s by these countries (with the exception of Iran) the mission contracts have been changed to advisory status.

In Poland Mi–2s on agricultural operations have an average utilisation of 500 flight hours per year.

Chapter 20

The last word

In the history of aviation there inevitably appear aerodynes, which are hailed as the last word in innovative design or performance. Some are things of sheer beauty like the Spitfire and the Concorde, while others are totally functional without any regard for elegance of line. In the latter category is the Russian Mi–V.12 helicopter, which is really an airliner fuselage with two Mi–6 engine pods and rotor systems mounted on outriggers. This mighty lifter seemed to many to be the last word in rotary-wing aircraft, but looks like losing its title to the Piasecki Heli-Stat.

Rusian Mi–V.12 heavy-lift helicopter

Frank Piasecki is a pioneer designer of tandem rotor helicopters and the Heli-Stat is his latest brain-child. It consists of four surplus Sikorsky S–58 helicopters rigidly connected to an ex-U.S. Navy helium-filled airship. One pilot in the left rear helicopter will fly the whole device via fly-by-wire system using micro-processors. The other three cockpits will each be manned by a flight engineer.

This is not a hare-brained scheme but the outcome of NASA wind-tunnel tests and mathematical models, and is even the subject of a navy operational requirement for a heavy lift aircraft. The challenge was responded to by a number of helicopter and airship manufacturers, but in 1980 the Piasecki Aircraft Corporation was awarded a ten million U.S. dollar contract by the U.S. Forest Service to provide a 25-ton (25-tonnes) vertical lift air vehicle.

The Forest Service's interest lies jointly in the ecology and economics of logging. Ground vehicles are limited to an economic range of one mile (1.6 km) from a road in timber country, and helicopters have much the same economic range. However, it is estimated that lighter-than-air vehicles could operate economically at haul distances of five miles (8 km) or more. The significance of this is that the average operable area of 3000 acres (1215 hectares) by a logging helicopter could probably be increased to 63 000 acres (25 500 hectares) by a lighter-than-air vehicle. Additionally there would be no need to cut the logs into lengths that could be handled by a helicopter.

The Heli-Stat when on the ground is nearly weightless, as the helium-filled envelope carries 99% of the weight of the helicopters and other systems. The helium lift figure of 99% allows 1% weight to simplify ground handling. The helicopters therefore are virtually free to lift nothing but payload. The payload of 25 tons (25 tonnes) for the prototype Heli-Stat is of course dictated by the type of helicopters used, but the potential is very much higher, and 160 tons (163 tonnes) has been forecast.

Piasecki Heli-Stat projected experiment heavy-lift aerostat

Completion of the 240 ft long (73.2 m) long Heli-Stat is planned for 1982, and technical assistance and programme management will be provided by the U.S. Naval Air Development Center with its expertise in airships.

The heavy construction industry is keeping a very interested watching brief on this project, as it is severely restricted in its very heavy lift demands by the limitations of existing helicopters. To even admit that helicopters have such limits in a book on commercial helicopters must indeed be the last word.

Civil helicopters — basic data

Notes:
  (i) The seating is shown as passengers/passengers + crew.
 (ii) The speed is the economical cruise/fast cruise at 1000 ft.
(iii) The range is the maximum distance that can be flown with full load at the maximum take-off weight quoted.

Robinson R22
Single piston-engine
2 seats
Speed 108 m.p.h.
Range 240 miles
Weight 1300 lb
Rotor diam. 25 ft 2 in

Brantly B2B
Single piston-engine
2 seats
Speed 85/100 m.p.h.
Range 250 miles
Weight 1670 lb
Rotor diam. 23 ft 9 in

Hughes 300
Single piston-engine
2/3 seats
Speed 85 m.p.h.
Range 250 miles
Weight 1900 lb
Rotor diam. 25 ft 4 in

Enstrom Shark
Single piston-engine
2/3 seats
Speed 100/110 m.p.h.
Range 290 miles
Weight 2350 lb
Rotor diam. 32 ft

Note: The earlier model F28A is similar to the Shark, but is 200 lb lighter and has a range of 200 miles.

Hiller 12
Single piston-engine
2/3 seats
Speed 90 m.p.h.
Range 225 miles
Weight 2800 lb
Rotor diam. 35 ft 5 in

Bell 47
Single piston-engine
2/3 seats
Speed 85 m.p.h.
Range 230 miles
Weight 2950 lb
Rotor diam. 37 ft 2 in

Hughes 500D
Single turbine-engine
4/5 seats
Speed 150/168 m.p.h.
Range 300 miles
Weight 3000 lb
Rotor diam. 26 ft 6 in

Bell Jet Ranger
Single turbine-engine
4/5 seats
Speed 130 m.p.h.
Range 350 miles
Weight 3200 lb
Rotor diam. 33 ft 4 in

Aerospatiale Alouette 2
Single turbine-engine
4/5 seats
Speed 110 m.p.h.
Range 300 miles
Weight 3527 lb
Rotor diam. 33 ft 6 in

Westland Gazelle
Single turbine-engine
4/5 seats
Speed 160 m.p.h.
Range 450 miles
Weight 3970 lb
Rotor diam. 34 ft 6 in

Bell Long Ranger
Single turbine-engine
6/7 seats
Speed 127/150 m.p.h.
Range 350 miles
Weight 4050 lb
Rotor diam. 37 ft

Aerospatiale Squirrel
Single turbine-engine
5/6 seats
Speed 133/150 m.p.h.
Range 460 miles
Weight 4190 lb
Rotor diam. 35 ft 1 in

Aerospatiale Twin Squirrel
Twin turbine-engines
5/6 seats
Speed 137/150 m.p.h.
Range 495 miles
Weight 4630 lb
Rotor diam. 35 ft 1 in

Aerospatiale Alouette 3
Single turbine-engine
6/7 seats
Speed 125 m.p.h.
Range 350 miles
Weight 4850 lb
Rotor diam. 36 ft 1 in

Note: The Lama is the 5-seat version of the Alouette 3, optimised for external load carrying.

Bolkow 105
Twin turbine-engines
4/5 seats
Speed 145 m.p.h.
Range 350 miles
Weight 5070 lb
Rotor diam. 32 ft 3 in

Agusta 109
Twin turbine-engines
7/8 seats
Speed 165/172 m.p.h.
Range 360 miles
Weight 5402 lb
Rotor diam. 36 ft 2 in

MBB-Kawasaki BK117
Twin turbine-engines
8/10 seats
Speed 138/170 m.p.h.
Range 340 miles
Weight 6173 lb
Rotor diam. 36 ft 11 in

Aerospatiale Dauphin
Single turbine-engine
9/10 seats
Speed 153/168 m.p.h.
Range 405 miles
Weight 6615 lb
Rotor diam. 37 ft 8¾ in

Aerospatiale Dauphin 2
Twin turbine-engines
9/10 seats
Speed 150/180 m.p.h.
Range 295 miles
Weight 7495 lb
Rotor diam. 38 ft 4 in

Bell 222
Twin turbine-engines
8/10 seats
Speed 145/170 m.p.h.
Range 480 miles
Weight 7850 lb
Rotor diam. 39 ft

Westland Whirlwind 3
Single turbine-engine
8/10 seats
Speed 104/110 m.p.h.
Range 300 miles
Weight 8000 lb
Rotor diam. 53 ft

Sikorsky S–62
Single turbine-engine
12/14 seats
Speed 98/105 m.p.h.
Range 460 miles
Weight 8100 lb
Rotor diam. 53 ft

Sikorsky S–76 Spirit
Twin turbine-engines
12/14 seats
Speed 145/167 m.p.h.
Range 460 miles
Weight 10 000 lb
Rotor diam. 44 ft

Bell 212
Twin turbine-engines
9/14 seats
Speed 125 m.p.h.
Range 300 miles
Weight 11 200 lb
Rotor diam. 48 ft

Bell 412
Twin turbine-engines
11/15 seats
Speed 150 m.p.h.
Range 380 miles
Weight 11 200 lb
Rotor diam. 46 ft

Sikorsky S–58T
Twin turbine-engines
16/18 seats
Speed 130 m.p.h.
Range 300 miles
Weight 13 000 lb
Rotor diam. 56 ft

Westland Wessex 60
Twin turbine-engines
12/17 seats
Speed 120 m.p.h.
Range 300 miles
Weight 13600 lb
Rotor diam. 56 ft

Aerospatiale 330J Puma
Twin turbine-engines
19/21 seats
Speed 155/160 m.p.h.
Range 340 miles
Weight 16315 lb
Rotor diam. 49 ft 3 in

Bell 214ST
Twin turbine-engines
17/19 seats
Speed 173 m.p.h.
Range 385 miles
Weight 16500 lb
Rotor diam. 52 ft

Sikorsky S–61N
Twin turbine-engines
26/30 seats
Speed 130 m.p.h.
Range 360 miles
Weight 20500 lb
Rotor diam. 62 ft

Boeing-Vertol Commercial Chinook
Twin turbine-engines
44/46 seats
Speed 153/165 m.p.h.
Range 575 miles
Weight 47000 lb
Rotor diam. 60 ft

Note: The Bell 214B Big Lifter has a single turbine-engine but can lift an external load of 8000 lb. With a rotor diam. of 50 ft it has a cruise speed of 153 m.p.h. over a range of 205 miles.

Navaids

Modern technology has provided the IFR helicopter with a bewildering variety to en-route navigation aids. These are examined with respect to their operational range, operational altitude, accuracy, and reliability. For off-shore operations the requirements are assessed as:
  (a) Operational Range: 300 nm from the shoreline, with adequate range along the shore-line.
  (b) Operational Altitude: 800 ft to 5000 ft.
  (c) Accuracy: ±4.0 nm with 95% probability.
  (d) Reliability: failure of one part of the total system, either ground or airborne, will not result in the complete loss of navigation.

(i) *Non-Directional Beacon (NDB)*
  (a) 15 nm to 75 nm.
  (b) Unlimited.
  (c) Indicator needle swing of an airborne Automatic Direction Finding (ADF) receiver must not exceed a total of ±10° anywhere within the usable distance required. The needle swing must not exceed ±5° during a standard approach to an airport.
  (d) Some NDB sites are equipped with dual transmitters.
Remarks: Stations normally operate in the frequency band 200 kHz to 415 kHz and transmit a continuous carrier signal with a 1020 Hz modulation keyed to provide identification.

(ii) *VHF Omni-Range (VOR)*
  (a) Limited by radio horizon effect.
  (b) At 800 ft the VOR signal is useful at a range of about 35 nm.
  (c) Bearing accuracy is ±3.5° (95% probability) relative to the desired centre line. The ±4.0 nm position error would be exceeded beyond 66 nm from the station, and would be ±12 nm at 200 nm.
  (d) At 800 ft there would have to be VOR stations ever 70 nm along routes to prevent loss of navigation capability.

(iii) *Tactical Air Navigation (TACAN)*
  (a) Limited by radio horizon effect.
  (b) At 800 ft useful signals available to 35 nm from the station.
  (c) Range accuracy is ±0.5 nm, or 3% of slant range, whichever is greater. Azimuth accuracy is 3.5° relative to the course centre line.

Beyond 65 nm the position error caused by bearing error would exceed 4.0 nm.

(d) At 800 ft an alternate station would have to be within 35 nm to preserve navigation capability.

(iv) *Multiple Distance Measuring Equipment (DME)*
(a) Limited by the radio horizon.

(b) Limited by the radio horizon.

(c) Distance measurement of ±0.5 nm (95% probability), or 3° of slant range, whichever is greater.

(d) Two DME stations must be within operational range of the aircraft for a position fix. For minimum reliability the aircraft would have to be within range of at least three DME stations at all times.

(v) *Doppler Navigation System*
(a) Unlimited.

(b) Unlimited.

(c) Degrades at a rate of 0.5 nm per hour along the track, and at 2% of distance travelled across track. At 300 nm the total error would exceed 6 nm.

(d) Dual installation would be required for necessary degree of reliability.

(vi) *Omega*
(a) Unlimited.

(b) Unlimited.

(c) Approximately 2 nm, but solar eruptions can cause unpredictable errors.

(d) Redundant transmitters provide an acceptable signal source. Dual receivers would provide a reliable airborne installation.

(vii) *Very Low Frequency (VLF) Communication Signals*
(a) Unlimited.

(b) Unlimited.

(c) Approximately 1.5 nm.

(d) Existing transmitters provide redundant signal sources, but the primary mission of the transmitters is for communication with the U.S. Navy fleet, so continuous availability cannot be assured.

(viii) *Loran-C*
(a) About 800 nm.

(b) Unlimited.

(c) 0.4 nm.

(d) May be poor unless redundant signal sources are provided. At present stations are located about 800 nm apart.

(ix) *Inertial Navigation System (INS)*
  (a) Unlimited.
  (b) Unlimited.
  (c) Accuracy decreases at a rate of 1 nm per hour of operation.
  (d) Requires two units in the aircraft, making the system very costly.

(x) *Global Positioning System (GPS)*
  (a) Unlimited.
  (b) Unlimited.
  (c) 30 ft or less.
  (d) Reliability should be good when 24 satellites are in place. Ground station failure will result in a slow degradation of system accuracy.

Note: This GPS, or NAVSTAR as it is sometimes called, will be a satellite based navigation system that is planned for completion by 1985. Although primarily a military system it will have some portion of its signal uncoded for civil use. It will have three groups of eight satellites in separate orbits.

Index

ABC (Advancing Blade Concept) 158, 159
Aberdeen 23
Accident rates 117, 118, 150
ADAC motorway patrol 89, 90
Advisory agencies 137
Aerodynamics 9, 10, 156
Agricultural aviation 31, 32, 33, 34, 35, 36, 165
Air ambulance 86, 87, 88
Air glaciers 97
Air logistic 20
Air taxi 109, 110, 111, 112
All-weather capability 74, 75, 76, 77, 156
Alouette, Aerospatiale 87, 120, 148, 170, 171
Analogue Training Computers 115
Antarctic 30
Anti-pollution 54
Archaeological survey 54
Autorotation 3, 12, 114

Baltimore City Police Department 82
Bank data transportation 54, 55
Bell 47 13, 33, 35, 84, 91, 127, 130, 170
Bolkow 105 42, 73, 120, 148, 172
Bristow Helicopters 19, 97
British Airways (British European Airways) Helicopters 99, 100, 101, 102, 103, 106
British Gas Corporation 41
British Helicopter Advisory Board 45, 95, 137, 143

Carson Helicopters 48, 64
China 30
Chinook, Boeing-Vertol 13, 29, 59, 60, 106, 108, 116, 130, 133, 174
Civil Helicopter Operations
  beginning 2
  comparison with fixed-wing operations 2, 3
Climatic effects 16
Commodore Helicopters 109
Comparative forms of transport 5, 6
Configurations, rotor 5, 157, 158
Continental Shelf Act 21
Corrosion 123

Costs
  direct operating 135, 136
  fixed 134
  running 135
Court Helicopters 45, 46
Crashworthiness 122, 153, 154
Crop spraying 31, 32, 33, 34, 35, 36
Customs surveillance 52

Dauphin 2, Aerospatiale 30, 108, 172
Development, technological 150

Engines 5, 121, 148, 159, 160
Enstrom 2, 72, 169
Erickson Air Crane 62
Error, pilot 119, 123, 124
European Helicopter Association 138
Evergreen Helicopters 69
Executive helicopter 71
  company ownership 71, 72, 73, 74
  corporate helipads 77
  cost effectiveness 6, 77, 78
  pilot 74
Exhaust pollution 131, 132

Fallout dispersal 55
Fibreglass 120, 151
Firefighting 83, 84, 85, 86
Fish shoal detection 49, 50
Fish stocking 50
Flight capabilities 7
  controls 8, 153, 156, 157
  instruction 112
  limitations 10, 11
  simulator 27, 28, 114, 115, 116
Forest Service, U.S. 86, 167
French Gendarmerie 82
Future, the 1990s 155, 160, 161

Gazelle, Westland 72, 77, 171
Gearboxes 120, 152, 154, 156
Geophysical survey 46, 47, 48, 49
Growth of industry 4

Harbour pilot ferrying 42, 44
Heavy lift capability 56, 57
   capacity 70
   in construction 61, 62, 63
   future 69
   pilot 70
   special tasks 64
   unusual tasks 67, 68, 69
Helicopter Association of America 137
Helicopter Club of America 145
Helicopter Club of Great Britain 143
Heli-Orient 91
Helipads, corporate 77
Heli-Stat 166, 167
High lift 67
High rise building rescue 92, 93, 94, 95
Hiller 12 33, 35, 61, 170
Hughes 500 122, 130, 153, 170
Human responsibilities 117, 122

Icing 16, 17, 27, 124
Industry
   growth 4
   pattern 4, 136
International Chamber of Shipping 44
Island Helicopter Corporation, New York
   108, 109

James Bay Project 15
Jet Ranger, Bell 2, 55, 71, 87, 127, 132, 170

Kansas City Police 79, 80
Key personnel 136, 137

Labrador Sea 30
Lama, Aerospatiale 85, 171
Law enforcement 79, 80, 81, 82, 83
Leasing
   dry 72
   wet 72
Life flight 87
Lighthouse relief 17
Lightning 10, 11
Limitations, flight 10, 11
Local authority duties 51, 52
Logging, aerial 65, 67
London Metropolitan Police 81, 82
Los Angeles Police 81, 83
Low cost helicopter 139, 140, 141

MADGE 26, 27, 29, 103
Maintenance, on condition 152, 153
Marketing 137
Markets

forecast usage 148, 149
potential growth 14, 15, 147, 148
ten year forecast 147
Maryland State Police 89
Mashman, Joe 91
MAST 87
Median line 24
Mi-V.12 59, 164, 166
Mission Aviation Fellowship 91
Motorway patrol 88, 89, 90
Mountain flying 18

Narcotics eradication 52, 53
NASA research programme 154, 155
National fleets 15
Navaids 25, 26, 28, 29, 175
New York Airways 99, 102, 103
New Zealand 35
Noise
   abatement 130, 131, 155, 156
   criteria and certification 128, 129
   measurement 126, 127, 128
   sources 130
North Sea oil and gas operations 21, 22, 23
   helicopter landing officers 25
   helicopter protected zones 24
   helideck standards 25
   IFR operations 26
   Navaids 25
   pilot training 24

Oil demand and supply 20, 28
   Atlantic Continental Shelf 29, 30
   Gulf of Alaska 28
   Gulf of Mexico 20, 21
   world-wide operations 30
Okanagan Helicopters 69

Performance 12, 13, 122
Personnel, key 136, 137
Petroleum Helicopters Inc. 20, 68
Photography, aerial 36, 37
Piasecki, Frank 166
Pilot error 119, 123, 124
Pipeline inspection 41
Polish helicopters 165
Powerline inspection 38, 39, 40
Powerplants/propulsion 5, 121, 148
Press coverage 37
Private helicopter 139
   pilot training 112, 113, 141, 142
Property selection 55
Puma, Aerospatiale 103, 108, 151, 174

Ranching 51
Railway police 83
Rappelling 82, 84, 85
Redifon Flight Simulation 115, 116
Rescue 90, 91, 92, 93
Research, NASA programme 155
Robinson R22 139, 140, 141, 149, 169
Rocky Mountain helicopters 85
Rolls-Royce engines 148
Rotor blades 120, 150, 151
Rotors, tail 121, 122, 152
Russian helicopters 86, 162, 163, 164

Sabena Helicopters 100
Safety on design 119, 120
Scheduled services 99, 100
    future prospects 105, 106, 107
    Greenland 104
    Scotland 104, 107, 108
    U.K. 100, 101, 102, 103, 104
    U.S.A. 102, 103, 104
SFO Helicopter Airlines 100, 103
Shellfishing 50
Ship resupply 45, 46
Sikorsky, Igor 1, 7, 57, 157, 161
Sikorsky S–58T 64, 173
Sikorsky S–61 6, 23, 24, 26, 27, 29, 100, 101,
    102, 103, 116, 174
Sikorsky S–64 Skycrane 57, 58, 59, 62, 69, 70
Sikorsky S–76 Spirit 5, 6, 73, 78, 120, 173
Simulator, flight 27, 28, 114, 115, 116
Slingload aerodynamics 59, 60, 61
Slope operations 19
Soloy conversions 70, 91
South America 30
Sport, helicopter 143

future prospects 146
    World Championships 143, 144, 145
Squirrel, Aerospatiale 72, 120, 171
Structures 156
Survey
    archaeological 54
    geophysical 46, 47, 48, 49
Swiss Air-Rescue 91

Tail rotors 121, 122, 152
Tandem rotors 5, 157
Technological development 150
T.V. coverage 38
Tilt rotor 159, 161
Tobias, Gerald 78
Trade Associations 137, 138
Training
    commercial pilot 113
    private pilot 112, 113
Transmissions 120, 152, 154, 156
Trucking monitoring 54
Turbomeca 121, 148
Turbulence 17, 18

U.S. Army 114, 154
U.S. Coast Guard 98

Vibration 132, 133, 153, 154

Wake turbulence 125
Water sampling 42
Weather radar 26
Whaling 49
Wildlife protection 50, 51

X-wing 159